SHARE

SHARE

DELICIOUS BOARDS FOR SOCIAL DINING

THEO A. MICHAELS
Foreword by Jean-Christophe Novelli

Photography by
Mowie Kay

DEDICATION

For Anna, Eva, Lex and Luca – love you x

Senior designer Sonya Nathoo
Editorial director Julia Charles
Production controller David Hearn
Art director Leslie Harrington
Publisher Cindy Richards

Food stylist Kathy Kordalis
Prop stylist Olivia Wardle
Indexer Hilary Bird

First published in 2020 by
Ryland Peters & Small
20–21 Jockey's Fields, London WC1R 4BW
and 341 E 116th St, New York NY 10029
www.rylandpeters.com

10 9 8 7 6 5 4 3 2

ISBN: 978-1-78879-211-0

Printed in China

A CIP record for this book is available from the British Library. US Library of Congress Cataloging-in-Publication Data has been applied for.

NOTES

· Both British (Metric) and American (Imperial plus US cups) measurements are included in these recipes for your convenience, however, it is important to work with one set of measurements only and not alternate between the two within a recipe.

· Ovens should be preheated to the specified temperatures. We recommend using an oven thermometer. If using a fan-assisted oven, adjust temperatures according to the manufacturer's instructions.

· All eggs are medium (UK) or large (US), unless specified as large, in which case US extra-large should be used. Uncooked or partially cooked eggs should not be served to elderly, young children, pregnant women or those with compromised immune systems.

· When a recipe calls for grated zest of citrus fruit, buy unwaxed fruit and wash well before using. If you can only find treated fruit, scrub well in warm, soapy water before using.

· Extra-virgin olive oil is the highest quality oil. It is unrefined, contains antioxidants and anti-inflammatories and has a low smoke point and heightened flavour. It is best used for dressings and drizzles. Refined olive oil is milder in flavour and contains less health benefits but its higher smoke point makes it good for cooking.

CONTENTS

FOREWORD BY JEAN-CHRISTOPHE NOVELLI

I first met Theo many years ago, when he came to my cookery school, The Novelli Academy, in my home, for a trial. Before he even had time to turn the pan on I realised, straight away, that he had a lot to offer. The way he presented his very well selected produce and the dexterity with which he handled things, immediately gave me satisfaction and pleasure watching him work; and I was right! Theo's cuisine is simply delicious.

I love his style and versatility, and the way he brings value to the produce, without any urgency, is just so appetizing. When Theo cooks he has a beautiful rhythm, which naturally exposes his passion and elegance. On top of that, Theo is incredibly amicable and has a very genuine nature, as well as being a dedicated family man. I am delighted to see Theo making a name for himself.

Because I enjoyed Theo's first book Orexi! so much, I offered to write the foreword for his next book; et voila! Here we are! This wonderful book is a reflection of himself and his origins, which is not about any desire to impress but to express and to share the simplicity and absolute pleasure of eating well.

Theo's new book is brilliant. What you would call a delightful sunny Mediterranean day – on a plate.

Jean Christophe

INTRODUCTION

I love a good sharing board. Over the past few years I've created hundreds of shared dining experiences, ranging from romantic boards for two, to vast, opulent banqueting tables that can feed 250 people, all varying in theme and style depending on the occasion, location and guests' preferences. Why do I love the concept so much? For me, it's an awe-inspiring moment when I see guests approaching a sharing table for the first time; it seems to tap into some long-buried primal hunter-gather instinct. It's truly interactive: they want to explore, to hunt for their food amongst all the tempting dishes available, take hold of their edible loot – it's the same reaction I see in my kids when they spot a pick 'n' mix!

My signature sharing boards were born at the very first event I worked on as Executive Chef for Elsewhere Events. I was asked to create a new dining experience that delivered great-tasting food in an exciting way, and boards were what I came up with. They're fun, bring people together and ultimately that is what motivates me and what is at the very heart of all the food I create – a desire to share delicious food with my family and friends, spend quality time together, have a laugh and create experiences and memories that will live on, not just end the minute you leave the dining table. Basically, to put the important stuff in life centre-stage through my cooking.

The sharing boards I've developed for you to enjoy are intended to recreate the same experience I literally bring to the table with my chef's hat on – albeit on a smaller scale. My food is designed to be presented straight onto a surface, keeping the use of serving dishes to a minimum (where practical), so effectively laying out the food as one huge platter, or canvas (if you want to consider yourself something of an artist...). Your guests select what they want and serve themselves straight from the board. Once laid out, my themed menus will generate a buzz of excitement, create a sense of plenty and abundance and, most importantly, bring everyone together around the table to enjoy a sociable, shared dining experience. All the recipes included will also work as stand-alone dishes, so I suggest you pick some you like the sound of and try them out first as quick midweek suppers or more leisurely weekend meals. Then, bring a menu together as one impressive sharer to see how the recipes all come together to create something more than the sum of its parts. Here's a little summary of what to expect:

SIMPLE Sometimes life is just too short to be stuck in the kitchen while your friends are having a jolly in the room next door... This simple idea is all about making feeding people as easy as possible. Simply buy in what you fancy from the deli counter – charcuterie, cheeses, prepared antipasti dishes, good olives, etc. and add salad stuff, fruit and good bread. Lay it all out to create a tempting grazing board; perfect to serve as a relaxed lunch or an evening gathering where wine and conversation need to flow uninterrupted.

BRUNCH I am a big fan of brunch; mainly because it's early enough in the day to just eat something light, but late enough to ensure that throwing back an eye-popping Bloody Mary isn't frowned upon! Win win. My menu offers a delicious selection of hot and cold recipes to cater to everyone's cravings – whether you are feeding a sleepy head who just wants a zingy fruity yogurt pot to wake them up or those in need of some seriously substantial fuel to get their day started.

MEZE I'm of Greek Cypriot heritage so for me this is, of course, the original and best sharing board. It offers a selection of mouth-watering dishes inspired by traditional recipes cooked across Greece and the Mediterranean. Choose from a variety of moreish dips and souvlaki skewers, hot from the grill, ready to be wrapped in homemade flatbreads and eaten with all the tasty trimmings. The added benefit here is that there are no plates on the board to smash...

GARDEN Veganism is becoming hugely popular and so offering a plant-based board in this book was a no-brainer. My 'garden' board is packed with flavour as well as intriguing recipes, designed to stimulate the eye as well as the appetite, from my signature edible flower pots, to banana blossom tempura and 'no-bird' chicken pie (with a mystery ingredient...). This is a menu full of gastronomic delights that will keep even the most reluctant part-time vegan satisfied.

PICNIC My way of paying homage to the great British summertime, and one of it's most enduring traditions. Shake out your plaid blankets and get the wicker hamper packed – we are going on a picnic! Here you'll find my favourite family-day-out recipes, ranging from shrimp and potted crab, satisfying spinach and feta quiche and a ridiculously refreshing cucumber salad with a Pimm's dressing. Finish up with a summer berry terrine and chamomile shortbread to dunk into a home-made lemon and thyme curd. The only thing you're missing is the wasps...

OCEAN This magnificent sharing menu brings together a host of edible treasures from the surf. My recipes take you on a culinary voyage of discovery, from lightly pickled swordfish and Vietnamese squid salad, to baked langoustines with a melting black garlic butter and then, finally, we cruise back home with an East End of London classic from my childhood; prawns/shrimp, cockles and whelks in vinegar. All served with a fennel and green apple salad on the side, as refreshing as a dip in the ocean on a sweltering day.

BARBECUE For me, a barbecue with family and friends is always an informal occasion, so serving everything on a board feels exactly right. Cooking over fire is something primal that I am passionate about, so in the spirit of sharing the love, I've brought you a selection of recipes for an outdoor grill, ranging from simple to sophisticated. My Greek-style lamb chops and blackened mackerel with gremolata both celebrate the pared-back elegance of Mediterranean cooking (my main culinary influences growing up), while the lemongrass-marinated steaks, charred Caesar salad and vibrant pico de gallo salsa are all tasty recipes that blew my mind later in life when I first tasted them on my travels around the globe, and share with you now.

HARVEST This board literally screams autumn/fall and celebrates the best of comfort food as the days draw in and the temperature falls. Whole roasted pumpkins and squash are hollowed out and used as ingenious serving vessels for a range of hearty and warming casseroles, from pork and mulled cider to smoky chicken and black bean. Serve with my skillet cornbread studded with Padron peppers and a platter of griddled pears, chicory and melting blue cheese.

FEAST Celebrating a special occasion? Or just in need of a bit of self-indulgence... then this is the board for you. Feast offers up an array of rich, opulent dishes from a side of coffee-glazed salmon and a slow-cooked pork belly with a rich roasted apple ketchup to luxurious roasted vegetables. It's big and bold and will ensure no one goes hungry and everyone feels loved.

SWEET The ultimate indulgence – an entire sharing board comprised of desserts and sweet treats that boasts an array of colours, flavours and textures to tantalize even the sweetest tooth; a perfect pavlova dripping with syrupy poached plums, a dark chocolate tablet studded with dried cherries and pistachios and spiced with turmeric, a tangy citrus salad, drenched in a rosewater caramel... food for the hedonist in all of us!

SIMPLE

HOW TO BUILD A SHARING BOARD

You can follow these stages when building any of the boards in this book, and while my Simple share (check out page 17) is all about the convenience of buying in what you need, I couldn't resist adding a couple of easy but delicious recipes to include (see opposite).

CHOOSE YOUR BOARD Over the years I've used a lot of surfaces as boards – I've even improvised with doors and floor tiles (new of course!). You can't beat a wooden chopping board for a small sharer or a piece of plywood for something larger. If you rub olive oil into the wood this helps protect the surface from staining. When you are including oily or juicy food, a non-porous surface like slate, glass or ceramic works best. But as long as what you choose is clean, food-safe and heat-proof, if necessary, you're good to go!

START BIG Boards work best when they have a few visual 'anchors' – big pieces of food that add structure and give definition. These can be larger cuts of meat, sides of fish or wheels of cheese. Depending on the size of the board you are creating, aim for one, three or five centrepieces placed asymmetrically on the board.

CLUSTERS Once the big stuff is in place, you can start to fill the spaces in between with groups of smaller produce, such as a handful of fresh figs or apricots, some mounds of olives, a handful of salad leaves, etc.

COLOURS Consider colours carefully. Use shades that work with your theme (such as my Harvest board). Or, if your board is all one type of food and seems a bit flat, take a step back and see where you could use a bursts of colour to liven it up, then dot clusters of brightly coloured food, usually fresh produce, all around it.

HEIGHT Think about height; it's good to have some variation; if your board is big enough, slide smaller boards under some things to add height, or stack up wheels of cheese and add a pile of overhanging grapes. If your board is large enough, candlesticks can add drama but avoid dripping wax – faux ones are useful.

FILLERS The board will start to fill at this point, so now is when you move to the smaller pieces; a handful of dates or nuts squeezed in some of the gaps. Arrange lines of layered crackers; these can also act as useful barriers between, say, cheese and cold meats.

FINALE No sharing board is complete without garnishes. I've never been a fan of a grazing table where there are bits you're not sure you can eat. No one wants to start chewing on a eucalyptus leaf... I use sprigs of fresh herbs, halved citrus fruits and pomegranates and edible flowers. Finally, choose something you can drizzle – use it to fill in tiny gaps and add movement and fun to the board. More often than not I use a sticky balsamic glaze or you could try my vibrant coloured syrups on page 156.

MY TOP 5 TIPS

1. Build your board bearing in mind that it will be seen from all sides by your guests.
2. Odd numbers work best for visual displays so arrange smaller things in groups of three, five and so on.
3. Keep wet ingredients away from dry – don't put your melon next to the crackers!
4. Place condiments and accompaniments conveniently close; so cheese next to chutney, ham next to mustard.
5. Keep all the garnishes edible to avoid confusion, embarrassment and possible food poisoning!

GRIDDLED APRICOTS WITH LAVENDER & BEE POLLEN

I first made a variation of these as a last-minute hors d'oeuvre when working in France and loved the subtle floral note of the lavender alongside the cheese and apricot. Griddling the apricots changes their texture and flavour and adds a slight caramel note to the flesh.

MAKES 10

5 small, ripe fresh apricots
125-g/4½-oz. log soft creamy soft goat's cheese
2 tablespoons clear runny honey
1 tablespoon dried culinary quality lavender
1 tablespoon bee pollen (optional)

Halve the apricots, remove the stone/pit and cut away any dark patches by the stalk. Griddle the apricots cut-side down on a smoking hot griddle pan to create a few charred lines. This only takes a minute; you're not cooking the apricot, just giving it a little flavour and colour from the griddle pan.

With the apricots sitting skin-side down, spoon 1 heaped teaspoon of goat's cheese across the centre, neatening it with your fingers, if need be. Drizzle a few fine lines of honey across the top and finish with a small pinch of lavender and bee pollen (if using).

Note: A few larger sprigs of lavender make a nice garnish when arranged around these griddled apricots on your board.

FRESH FIGS WITH GOAT'S CHEESE & HONEY

It goes without saying you want to use figs that are ripe, soft and sweet here. I really enjoy them with goat's cheese and I am sure you will too.

MAKES 12

3 fresh figs, quartered lengthways
125-g/4½-oz. log soft, creamy goat's cheese
1 tablespoon clear runny honey
1 tablespoons edible dried flowers (optional)
sea salt flakes and cracked black pepper, to season

Open each fig quarter slightly, then push 1 teaspoonful of the goat's cheese into the centre. Drizzle with just a few fine lines of honey, add a pinch of flowers (if using) and a light seasoning of salt and pepper.

FOODS TO INCLUDE IN A SIMPLE SHARE

Building a simple sharing board is a great way
to get started. It's based on buying in what you need
rather than cooking dishes from scratch. Focusing on
a theme really helps give a simple board like this a nice
narrative. It could be based on the provenance of the
foods, for example; I often like to use just British
cheeses and cured meats, but you could stick
to an Italian-style board with antipasti dishes, or opt
for Spanish tapas-style nibbles. Pick and choose what
you fancy from my list of suggestions, but don't
be limited by it – it's your board after all!

CHEESE

A selection of cheeses (about 750 g/1 lb 11 oz. total
weight will serve 8 people). Choose one cheese to act
as a centrepiece on the board and then add in a few
smaller pieces around it. For a variety of tastes and
textures, try to include one each of the following:

• Hard cheese, such as pecorino or manchego
• Medium cheese, such as cave-aged Cheddar
• Soft cheese, such as Camembert or Brie
• Blue cheese, such as Stilton or Shropshire Blue
• Goat's cheese, either a soft chevre or a hard cheese;
whatever your preference, or even a fresh burrata

COLD MEATS

An assortment of cured meats (allow about 150 g/
6 oz. of sliced meats per person), cooked ham and pâté.

• Serrano ham, sliced
• Parma ham, sliced
• Salami, either sliced or whole
• Chorizo, either sliced or whole
• a cooked ham (about 300 g/11 oz.)
• a coarse rustic or smooth pâté (about 150 g/ 6 oz.)

FRUITS AND VEGETABLES
• red and/or green seedless grapes
• pomegranates
• fresh figs
• honeydew melon slices (skin on)
• Medjool dates
• fresh or dried apricots
• a variety of tomatoes, fresh and sun-dried
• celery sticks (leaves on)
• a few handfuls of fresh rocket/arugula

BREADS AND CRACKERS
• sourdough bread, ripped into bite-sized pieces and
drizzled with olive oil
• breadsticks; plain, seeded or flavoured with olives etc.
• a variety of good crackers and biscuits for cheese,
such as sourdough, charcoal, rye etc.

NIBBLES AND CONDIMENTS
• marinated green and/or black olives
• cornichons
• pickled onions
• caper berries
• pistachio nuts
• salted almonds
• tomato, caramelized onion or any other vegetable
or fruit chutney
• Spanish quince paste (membrillo)
• wholegrain mustard

DRIZZLES AND GARNISHES
• fresh honeycomb
• balsamic glaze
• pomegranate molasses or date molasses
• sprigs of fresh herbs
• pesticide-free edible flowers and petals

BRUNCH

BLOODY MARIA

No brunch would be complete without a little tipple and
this fusion of two drinks I love, Tequila (misspent youth) and
a Bloody Mary (misspent adulthood) is my go-to when drinking
before midday... I like to serve it in a large Kilner jar to share,
but you can make in a jug/pitcher and pour if preferred.

SERVES 6

200 ml/7 fl. oz. silver tequila
400 ml/14 fl. oz. tomato juice
freshly squeezed juice of 2 limes
½ tablespoon Worcestershire sauce
Tabasco sauce, to taste
fresh horseradish, to taste
a few pinches of celery salt

freshly ground black pepper,
   to taste
celery spears, leaves on
a large red fresh chilli/chile
2 limes, cut into wedges
ice cubes

a large kilner jar or jug/pitcher
drinking straws

Half-fill a large Kilner jar or jug/pitcher with ice cubes and add the tequila,
tomato juice, lime juice and Worcestershire Sauce. Stir, season to taste with
Tabasco, horseradish, celery salt and black pepper and stir until chilled.
Garnish with the celery spears and chilli/chile. Either add straws and serve
as a sharer or pour into individual ice-filled glasses, garnished with lime.

ROSÉ-ROASTED RHUBARB & PISTACHIO YOGURT POTS

There is something rather sensuous about eating a creamy yogurt for brunch. Here, the sour-sweet rhubarb caresses the pale curves making them very compatible bedfellows; add some pistachios for the perfect ménage à trois.

MAKES 6 SMALL SERVINGS

400 g/14 oz. forced rhubarb
90 g/½ scant cup caster/granulated sugar
12 cardamom pods, lightly cracked
125 ml/½ cup rosé wine
½ teaspoon freshly squeezed lemon juice
500 g/2⅓ cups thick Greek yogurt
crushed pistachio kernels and edible flowers,
   to garnish

Preheat the oven to 180°C (350°F) Gas 4.

Cut the rhubarb into 2.5-cm/1-inch pieces and toss them in a small roasting pan with the sugar, cardamom pods, wine and lemon juice. Cover securely with foil and stab half a dozen small holes in the foil.

Bake in the preheated oven for 20 minutes, until tender, then remove from the heat and leave to cool. Once cooled, decant into a sterilized jar and leave in the fridge overnight to give the cardamom and wine time to infuse the rhubarb.

When ready to assemble, divide the yogurt between six small serving glasses or bowls. Place a tablespoon of roasted rhubarb (removing and discarding the cardamom pods) on top of each along with another tablespoon of the liquid. Sprinkle over some pistachios and garnish with an edible flower.

BLUEBERRY, COCONUT & CHIA SEED MINI AÇAI BOWLS

I first came across açai in the 1990s on Ilha Grande, an island just off the Brazilian coast. After a few caipirinhas the night before, a bowl of açai was the best way to kickstart the day. Packed with goodness, it has a chocolately note which marries well with the chia and coconut.

MAKES 6 SMALL SERVINGS

3 small bananas
300 g/1 cup pure açai berry pulp
500 g/2⅓ cups thick Greek yogurt
3 tablespoons toasted chia seeds
6 tablespoons toasted coconut flakes
fresh blueberries and edible flowers, to garnish

Peel the bananas and mash the flesh with a fork, then whip it into as smooth a pulp as you can manage. Add the açai pulp and mix until thoroughly combined.

Divide the yogurt between six small serving bowls, then top each with a few tablespoons of the banana and açai mixture.

Top with generous sprinkles of toasted chia seeds and coconut flakes and add some fresh blueberries to finish (halved if they are a little on the large side). Add an edible flower to garnish, if you like.

FRENCH TOAST WITH ALL THE TRIMMINGS

This is a staple brunch dish in the bedlam that is a morning in the Michaels' household. Easier to make than pancakes (and less messy when the kids 'help') but just as tasty. Serve hot with all the trimmings – a few berries and lashings of maple syrup. They will go quickly!

MAKES 4 SLICES

12 rashers/slices smoked pancetta
4 just-ripe bananas
butter, for cooking
4 eggs

4 large slices of thick-cut white bread
pure maple syrup, for drizzling
salt and freshly ground black pepper
any fresh berries, to serve
icing/confectioners' sugar, to dust
    (optional)

Preheat the oven to 200°C (400°F) Gas 6.

Line a baking sheet with baking parchment. Arrange the strips of pancetta on top of a sheet of baking parchment and then lay a second sheet of baking parchment over the top, pat it down to stick to the pancetta and then pop it into the preheated oven for 10 minutes, or until the pancetta is cooked and crispy. (Placing the baking parchment on top helps to keep the rashers/slices flat.)

Try to buy bananas that are just ripe because if they are too soft they tend to break up in the pan. Peel them and cut in half lengthways. Heat a knob/pat of butter in a frying pan/skillet and, once it's melted, lay the bananas in the pan, cut-side down. Fry them for a few minutes until they have turned slightly golden and you can smell them. Carefully turn them over using a fish slice and cook for a few minutes more, before removing them from the pan and setting aside.

Pour away any excess butter from the pan, but don't wipe it.

Whisk the eggs in a wide-rimmed bowl and season lightly with salt and pepper. Working with one slice of bread at a time, dip it into the beaten eggs letting it soak for a few seconds, then coat the other side of the bread before laying it into the hot pan to cook for a few minutes on each side. Repeat until all of your bread is transformed into French toast.

Top each slice of toast with crispy pancetta and a few slices of fried banana. Drizzle maple syrup over the top, letting it meander down the sides, and add a few fresh berries, then add a little dusting of icing/confectioners' sugar, if you fancy it.

SMOKY AUBERGINE SHAKSHUKA

I make a version of this for brunch for our guests at a beautiful Chateau in Provence, France, and it never fails to satisfy that mid-morning craving for something a little spicy. Serve with toasted sourdough and joie de vivre! If you don't have a large enough skillet, you can simply divide the mixture and cook it in two smaller pans.

SERVES 3 AS A MAIN, 6 AS A SHARER

1 aubergine/eggplant
1 small onion, diced
1 garlic clove, finely sliced
1 tablespoon ras el hanout
½ teaspoon smoked paprika
1 tablespoon tomato purée/paste
1 teaspoon sugar
500 ml/2 cups tomato passata

6 eggs
50 g/2 oz. feta, crumbled
a handful of fresh coriander/cilantro
   leaves, roughly chopped (optional)
fresh red or green chilli/chile, sliced
olive oil, for frying and drizzling
salt and freshly ground black pepper

*a 25-cm/10-inch ovenproof frying
   pan/skillet*

Preheat the oven to 200°C (400°F) Gas 6.

Cut the aubergine/eggplant in half lengthways, then quarter each half to create eight full-length wedges. Fry the aubergine/eggplant wedges in a hot ovenproof frying pan/skillet with a generous glug of olive oil for 5 minutes on each side, until browned. Remove them from the pan and set aside.

Add the onion to the pan with a little more olive oil and fry for 5 minutes, then add the garlic and cook for 1 minute more. Add the ras el hanout, smoked paprika, tomato purée/paste and sugar and stir in. Follow with the tomato passata and season well with salt and pepper. Arrange the aubergine/eggplant wedges in the sauce and leave to simmer for 5–10 minutes, after which time taste the sauce, adjust the seasoning to taste and remove the pan from the heat.

Make six small gaps inbetween the curled aubergine/eggplant wedges and crack the eggs, allowing a little of the white to fall away, then pour the eggs into the gaps. Sprinkle over half the feta, drizzle with olive oil and place the pan in the preheated oven for 7 minutes for medium-cooked eggs.

Remove from the oven, drizzle with a little more olive oil, scatter over the coriander/cilantro, remaining feta and chilli/chile slices and add a pinch of salt. Serve with toasted sourdough bread on the side to mop up the juices.

OUZO-CURED SALMON

Homecuring seems steeped in mystery but it's really so easy – a few days in the fridge, yes, but the preparation is quick. It's great to have on standby for impromptu brunches. Either slice it into pieces ready to go, or keep it whole for people to carve for themselves and eat with toasted bagels with a cream cheese and horseradish whip.

MAKES 12 SERVINGS

200 g/1 cup white granulated sugar
100 g/½ cup demerara sugar
400 g/2 cups coarse sea salt
1 side of fresh salmon (about 1 kg/
   2 lb. 4 oz.), deboned, skin on
60 ml/¼ cup ouzo
a small handful of freshly chopped dill

SPICE MIX
2 star anise

12 cloves
1 tablespoon fennel seeds
1 tablespoon coriander seeds
4 bay leaves

TO GARNISH AND SERVE
4 tablespoons cream cheese
4 tablespoons horseradish sauce
a little freshly squeezed lemon juice
freshly ground black pepper
large caper berries and dill flowers
plain bagels, lightly toasted

Grind up the spice mix ingredients using a pestle and mortar or if you don't have one, in a plastic bag by giving it a good bash with the bottom of a saucepan! Combine this mix with both the sugars and salt – this is your dry curing mixture.

Take a large roasting pan (with high sides and big enough to take the salmon laid out flat) and sprinkle about a quarter of the dry curing mixture over the base of it, roughly where the fish will lay. Lay the salmon, skin-side down, in the pan and drizzle over the ouzo, massaging it into the flesh with your fingers.

Sprinkle the rest of the dry curing mixture over the fish, trying to completely cover the top and sides and pat it down. Take a sheet of clingfilm/plastic wrap and place over the fish, tucking it in around the edges as much as possible, then cover the fish again with another sheet of clingfilm/plastic wrap.

Place a small chopping board or baking sheet on top of the fish, ensuring the edges of it fit inside the roasting pan. Pop the whole thing in the fridge, weighing down the chopping board or baking sheet with a few food cans, you need this to be fairly heavy.

Leave in the fridge for a minimum of two days, ideally three. Periodically, once a day should do it, pour away the juices that start to expel from the fish (no need to remove all the clingfilm/plastic wrap, just open a gap in one corner to pour the liquid away whilst holding the fish in place).

After a few days, remove the fish from the pan wiping away as much of the curing mixture from the fish as possible. The fish should be nice and firm by now. Rinse the fish under cold water to remove all traces of the cure.

Pat dry with paper towels and cover the flesh side of the salmon with finely chopped dill and pat it down to help it stick. Carve thin slices of the salmon, starting at the tail end and carving at an angle towards the tail.

Take the cream cheese and horseradish and simply mix the two together with a few drops of lemon juice and a few grinds of black pepper to make a tasty whip.

When you're ready to serve, lightly toast some sliced bagels, spread a dollop of the cream cheese and horseradish whip over each side and top with a couple of slithers of the salmon. Garnish with large caper berries and dill flowers.

You can store the remaining salmon in the fridge wrapped in baking parchment after you've had your fill. I recommend carving it to order to stop the salmon drying out. It should keep for up to 5 days in the fridge.

SMOKED HADDOCK ON SOURDOUGH

If anything epitomizes an indulgent brunch it's got to be a combination of flaked smoked haddock, topped with a poached egg and a blanket of slightly sharp yet creamy sauce. Here, I make use of the poaching milk from the fish to create a light but no less delicious faux hollandaise.

MAKES 4 TOASTS

400 g/14 oz. smoked, undyed haddock
about 500 ml/2 cups full-fat/whole milk
1 dried bay leaf
4 slices of sourdough bread
a generous pinch of dried chilli flakes/
    hot red pepper flakes (optional)
12 spears fresh asparagus

1 tablespoon butter
1 tablespoon plain/all-purpose flour
½ teaspoon English/hot mustard
½ teaspoon cider vinegar
4 eggs or 12 quail's eggs, as preferred
freshly chopped flat-leaf parsley,
    to garnish
salt and freshly ground black pepper
olive oil, for brushing

Put the haddock in a snug-fitting saucepan and pour in enough milk to cover. Add a few grinds of black pepper and the bay leaf. Poach on a low simmer for about 5 minutes, until the flesh is opaque. Leave the fish in the milk until cool before removing it. Set aside and reserve the poaching milk.

Brush the sourdough bread with olive oil, season and sprinkle with a pinch of chilli/hot red pepper flakes (if liked). Lightly oil the asparagus. Heat a griddle/grill pan until really hot. Add the bread and toast for 2 minutes on each side, warming the asparagus in the pan at the same time until lightly browned and nutty.

Set a small saucepan over a low heat. Add the butter and flour and heat for 2 minutes or so to cook out the flour, then whisk in 125 ml/½ cup of the reserved poaching milk. Bring to a simmer, continuously whisking until you have a smooth, creamy sauce, adding more milk to achieve your desired consistency. Add the mustard and vinegar, stir, taste for seasoning, and set to one side until needed.

Next, poach your eggs in a pan of hot (but not boiling) water for about 5 minutes. Place the toasted sourdough slices on a serving board with the flaked fish and asparagus arranged on top, add the soft poached eggs and pour over as much faux hollandaise sauce as you fancy. Sprinkle some freshly chopped parsley over the top to garnish and add a grinding or two of black pepper.

MEZE

FETA TZATZIKI

Tzatziki is almost mandatory for any meze and it can take various forms; some are flavoured with dill, others mint, or even diced or grated cucumber... here is my personal preference.

MAKES 1 BOWL TO SHARE

½ cucumber
½ teaspoon salt, plus
   extra to taste
250 g/1¼ scant cups thick
   Greek yogurt
freshly squeezed juice
   of ½ lemon

4 tablespoons freshly
   chopped mint, plus
   a few leaves to garnish
1 garlic clove, crushed
2 tablespoons olive oil
4 tablespoons crumbled
   feta, plus extra to serve
a pinch of cayenne
   pepper, to garnish

Trim the ends off the cucumber then cut it in half lengthwise. Use a spoon to scoop out the watery seeds and discard. Leave the cucumber unpeeled and grate the flesh into a sieve/strainer. Fold in the salt and leave it to sit over a bowl for 10 minutes. Use your hands to squeeze as much moisture from the grated cucumber as possible and transfer the flesh into a clean bowl. (You need about 150 g/1 scant cup of cucumber flesh.)

Add the yogurt, lemon juice, mint, garlic and half the olive oil to the bowl with the cucumber and stir to combine. Taste and add a little salt if you think it needs it. Once fully combined, fold in the feta – I like to add the feta at this stage so it doesn't break up too much.

Finally transfer the tzaziki directly onto your sharing board or spoon it into a bowl. Garnish with a sprinkle of feta crumbs, drizzle over the remaining olive oil and add a pinch of cayenne pepper. A few fresh mint leaves for garnishing wouldn't go amiss either.

CREAMY BUTTER BEAN DIP

This delicious garlicky dip makes a great alternative to hummus and is quick and easy to make. Use the best quality butter/lima beans you can find – the ones you buy in a jar rather than in a can have a more velvety texture, which is what we want here, but canned work well too.

MAKES 1 BOWL TO SHARE

400-g/14-oz jar or can
   cooked butter/lima
   beans (235 g/1½ cups
   drained)
60 ml/¼ cup olive oil,
   plus extra for drizzling
1 garlic clove, crushed
freshly squeezed juice of

½ lemon
½ teaspoon salt
2 tablespoons freshly
   chopped flat-leaf
   parsley
1 finely diced preserved
   lemon and a pinch each
   of dried chilli/hot red
   pepper flakes and dried
   oregano, to garnish

Add the butter/lima beans, olive oil, garlic, lemon juice, salt and 1 tablespoon water to a food processor and blend until almost smooth – a little coarseness is quite nice. (If you prefer, put the ingredients in a bowl and use a hand-held stick blender to do this.) Once blended, add the chopped parsley and fold it in by hand. Taste and adjust the seasoning if necessary.

Spoon a couple of dollops of the dip directly onto your board and use the back of a spoon to make a swirl. Garnish with a sprinkle of the preserved lemon pieces, chilli/hot red pepper flakes, oregano and a little drizzle of olive oil.

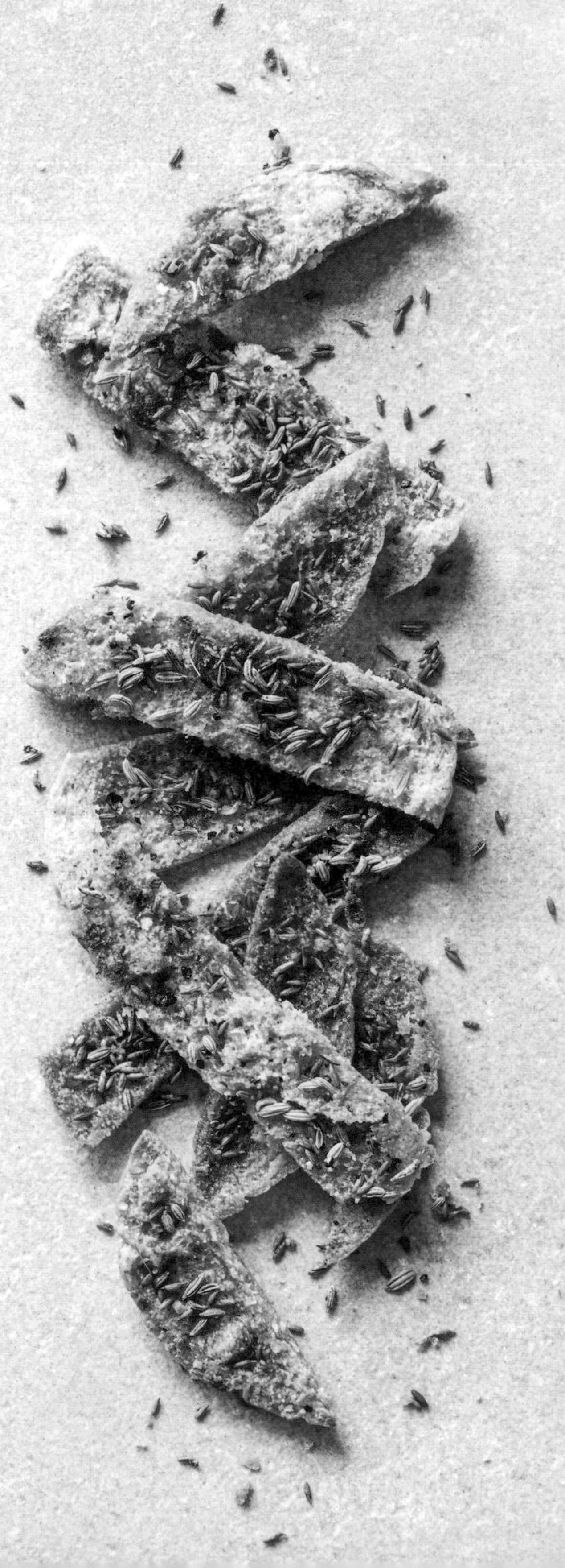

FENNEL SEED & SEA SALT PITA CHIPS

These are so easy to make that I actually feel guilty calling it a recipe but they taste so good you'll forgive me! The combination of smoky paprika, zingy fennel seeds and spicy heat make them terribly moreish and ideal for mopping up the delicious dips on your meze board.

MAKES ABOUT 40

4 store-bought pita breads
60 ml/¼ cup olive oil
½ teaspoon smoked paprika
½ teaspoon mild or hot chilli/chili powder
1 teaspoon cumin seeds
½ tablespoon sea salt flakes
freshly ground black pepper, to taste

Preheat the oven to 200°C (400°F) Gas 6.

Pitas have a natural pocket so split each pita to give you two whole sides of pita and stack them on top of each other. Use a large sharp knife to cut them widthwise into 5-cm/2-inch strips.

Put the pita strips in a large mixing bowl, drizzle over the olive oil. Add all the remaining ingredients and toss until the pita strips are well coated in oil and seasoning.

Arrange the pita strips on a large baking sheet and sprinkle over any leftover spices from the bowl. Bake in the preheated oven for about 12 minutes, or until crisp.

Remove from the oven and leave to cool before arranging them on your board, within easy reach of the delicious dips.

SPICED BUTTERNUT PIES

These are inspired by my Yiayia's pumpkin and raisin pies (their Cypriot name is *kolokotes*). Mine are filled with roasted butternut squash mixed with warming aromatic spices, studded with sweet dried cherries and encased in a simple shortcrust pastry.

MAKES ABOUT 8 SMALL PIES/TURNOVERS

500 g/1 lb. 2 oz. butternut squash
30 g/1 oz. white onion, diced
a pinch of ground cloves
a pinch of ground cumin
a generous pinch of ground cinnamon
olive oil, to drizzle
40 g/scant ¼ cup bulgur wheat
40 g/scant ⅓ cup dried cherries, chopped

400 g/14 oz. ready-made shortcrust pastry
1 egg, beaten with a splash of milk
1 tablespoon nigella seeds
1 tablespoon dried chilli/hot red pepper flakes
sea salt flakes, to sprinkle
Feta Tzatziki, to serve (page 34)

a baking parchment-lined baking sheet

Preheat the oven to 200°C (400°F) Gas 6.

To make the filling, peel, and dice the squash and cut it into 1-cm/³/8-inch cubes. Put the squash cubes and onion on a baking sheet with all the spices. Drizzle with olive oil and toss with your hands to coat the vegetables with oil and seasoning. Cook in the preheated oven for about 20 minutes, or until the squash is fork tender, the remove from the oven. Reduce the oven to 180°C (350°F) Gas 4.

To prepare the bulgur wheat, place it in a heatproof mixing bowl and pour in just enough boiling water to cover. Place a plate on top and leave the grains to hydrate and fluff up. Once the bulgur has absorbed all the water, tip the cooked squash into the same bowl and add the dried cherries. Mix until combined.

Break the shortcrust pastry into eight pieces of roughly the same size and roll each one out on a lightly floured surface, until each one is about 12 cm/5 inches diameter. Put 1–2 heaped tablespoons of filling on each disc fold the rest over and pinch along the edges to seal it in. Brush the egg and milk mixture over the pastry to glaze, then scatter a pinch of nigella seeds, dried chilli/hot red pepper flakes and sea salt over the top of each. Make as many as you can to use up the filling and pastry. Place on the lined baking sheet and bake in the preheated oven for 30 minutes, until golden. Serve warm with some Feta Tzatziki.

ONE-BITE GREEK SALAD ROLLS

I put these adorable one-bite Greek salads on the menu at my first pop-up restaurant night and they have been a crowd-pleaser ever since. Each one delivers all the components of a freshly made Greek salad in a single mouthful, making it perfect for your meze board.

MAKES ABOUT 15

2 cucumbers
100 g/3½ oz. feta cheese
10 baby plum tomatoes
a few pinches of dried oregano

10 Kalamata olives, pitted
½ red onion
a small bunch of fresh dill
about 3 tablespoons olive oil
2 tablespoons white wine vinegar
salt and freshly ground black pepper

This recipe is all about the prep and assembly.

Start with the cucumbers. Using a vegetable peeler, peel long strips of cucumber lengthways trying to get a little of the green skin on either side. Once the watery seeds start to appear, rotate the cucumber and peel from the other side. Lay all the slices out flat on a work surface and trim the ends with a sharp knife for a nice clean cut. Discard the seedy centre.

Cut the feta into batons about the same length as the width of your cucumber strips and about 1 cm/3/8 inch thick. Cut one piece for each strip of cucumber.

Cut the tomatoes into quarters, sprinkle over a little oregano and season with a few grinds of black pepper and a pinch of salt. To prepare the olives, cut them into quarters lengthwise, then finally, cut slivers of the red onion to match the size of the rest of the prepared ingredients.

To assemble the rolls, place a feta baton, olive, tomato wedge and red onion sliver at the top of a strip of cucumber and start rolling it towards you, once it's wrapped round a few times trim off any excess cucumber. Use your finger to dab a little olive oil onto the end of the cucumber to help it stick to itself. Turn the roll upright and repeat with the remaining cucumber strips. Garnish each with a small sprig of dill protruding from the top like a little green flag. Place them on the board in groups which helps them refrain from unwinding.

Just before serving, whisk together 2 tablespoons olive oil and the vinegar and drizzle a few drops of dressing onto each roll. Don't be tempted to dress them any earlier as they will start to wilt!

GYRO FLATBREADS

Gyros are the ultimate grab-and-go Greek street food; soft, chewy flatbreads wrapped snugly around charred meat, salad and always topped with fries – the trickle of juice and tzatziki down your chin is optional. The wraps used for gyros tend to be thicker than regular pitas and are much more pliable and seriously delicious. This recipe couldn't be easier or quicker – it's all about the ratios: one part milk to two parts self-raising/rising flour, a little olive oil and a pinch of salt.

MAKES 16 SMALL FLATBREADS

270 g/2 cups self-raising/rising flour, plus
   extra for dusting

250 ml/1 cup full-fat/whole milk
1 tablespoon olive oil
a pinch of salt

Mix all of the ingredients (except the flour for dusting) together in a bowl and work them together with your hands. Once the dough gets scraggy, tip it out onto a surface and start kneading by hand.

Once you've got a soft, slightly sticky dough, pop it back in the bowl, cover loosely with a kitchen cloth and leave to rest for 30 minutes (or if time is short, just charge on and don't bother resting it – it will still work out okay).

Cut the dough into 16 small pieces of equal size and roll each one out on a lightly floured surface until they are all about 5 mm/$\frac{1}{4}$ inch thick.

Heat a heavy-based frying pan/skillet until hot, then slap a flatbread down in it for a few minutes before flipping it over. Repeat and cook each gyro until golden brown on both sides. Stack them up and cover with a clean kitchen cloth to keep them warm until you are ready to arrange them on your board.

SPICY CHICKEN SHAWARMA

My chicken shawarma is scented with allspice and smoked paprika and marinated in a vibrant yogurt mixture, bringing it all to the table for your gastronomic enjoyment! Using chicken thighs keeps the chicken moist and succulent, and grilling/broiling it this way gives you that smoky charring reminiscent of street food. Serve in gyro flatbreads with fresh salad accompaniments and Greek yogurt on the side, for everyone to help themselves as part of your meze board.

MAKES 6 SERVINGS

6 chicken thighs, boned, skin on
100 g/scant ½ cup thick Greek yogurt
grated zest and freshly squeezed juice of
   1 lemon
3 tablespoons olive oil
1 tablespoon smoked paprika
1 tablespoon ground allspice
1 fresh red chilli/chile, finely diced
2 garlic cloves, crushed
1 tablespoon dried oregano
salt and freshly ground black pepper
a few sprigs of fresh coriander/cilantro,
   to garnish

TO SERVE
Gyro Flatbreads, to serve (page 39)

ACCOMPANIMENTS (OPTIONAL)
1 red onion, finely sliced
leaves from a bunch of fresh flat-leaf
   parsley, chopped
½ head of iceberg lettuce, shredded
½ cucumber, finely diced
6 ripe tomatoes, diced
3 lemons, cut into wedges, for squeezing
125 ml/½ cup thick Greek yogurt

Preheat the grill/broiler to hot.

Cut two deep scores across the top of each chicken thigh.

Mix all the other ingredients (except the garnish) together in a non-reactive bowl to make the marinade. Add the chicken thighs, toss to coat, then cover and leave to marinate for 1 hour (or overnight) in the fridge. Remove the chicken from the fridge 30 minutes before you plan to cook it to take off the chill.

Remove the chicken thighs from the marinade and arrange skin-side up and a few inches apart on a lightly oiled roasting pan. Cook under the preheated grill/broiler for about 15 minutes, until the flesh is cooked through and the skin has charred and started to crisp, turning occasionally.

Once cooked, slice across each thigh into strips 2.5-cm/1-inch wide, season with salt and pepper. Pile up on flatbreads, garnish with coriander/cilantro sprigs and place on your board, alongside any accompaniments you are serving.

GARDEN

BAKED CASHEW 'CAMEMBERT' WITH GARLIC & ROSEMARY

This recipe is inspired by a baked vegan cheese that a mate of mine served as the first course at a vegan supper – it was a revelation to me, utterly delicious and full of umami flavour. If you're reading this Matt, thank you for the inspiration. And no, you aren't getting a free book...

MAKES 1 ROUND

110 g/1 cup cashew nuts
1 garlic clove, chopped
2 tablespoons rice flour
½ teaspoon salt
½ tablespoon apple cider vinegar
¼ teaspoon Marmite/yeast extract
a generous pinch of rosemary needles

TO GARNISH
olive oil, for drizzling
6 sprigs of fresh rosemary
2 garlic cloves, quartered lengthways
a pinch of sea salt flakes

an empty wooden Camembert box or a 12.5-cm/5-inch round cake pan, lined with baking parchment

Preheat the oven to 180°C (350°F) Gas 4.

Put the cashew nuts in a saucepan and add 500 ml/2 cups water. Set over heat, bring to the boil and cook for about 12 minutes. Drain off 375 ml/1½ cups cooking liquid (top this up with tepid water if you have less).

Put all of the remaining ingredients (except the rosemary needles) in a mixing bowl and add the cooked cashews. Pour in the reserved cooking liquid and blend using a hand-held stick blender until you have a smooth paste. Fold in the rosemary and pour the mixture into a clean saucepan, then set over a medium heat. Stirring constantly, simmer the mixture until it pulls away from the edges and thickens to form a thick paste, this should only take a couple of minutes.

Pour the mixture into the Camembert box or lined cake pan and drizzle over a little olive oil. Stud with the sprigs of rosemary and garlic quarters and season with sea salt flakes. Bake in the preheated oven for about 10–12 minutes, or until you see a slight crust form on top, and then remove.

Serve with slices of crusty bread and Roasted Rainbow Crudités (page 50) and eat whilst still warm and gooey.

BEETROOT HUMMUS

Adding roasted beetroot gives a slightly sweeter note to this vibrant pink hummus. It tastes luxurious but is incredibly easy to make, and to speed things up even more, I use ready-cooked beetroot, though you can roast and peel your own if you have more time.

MAKES 1 BOWL TO SHARE

300 g/10½ oz. cooked chickpeas/garbanzo beans
100 g/3½ oz. cooked beetroot/beet
2 garlic cloves
1 heaped tablespoon tahini
freshly squeezed juice of ½ lemon
1 teaspoon salt
2 tablespoons olive oil, plus extra to drizzle

TO FINISH
2 tablespoons toasted pine nuts/kernels
a pinch of sesame seeds, black and white (optional)
a handful of coarsely chopped flat-leaf parsley leaves

Simply put all the ingredients in a blender and blend to a smooth paste. (Note: You can pop your chickpeas out of their skins too, for an even smoother hummus.) You may need to add a splash of water to loosen it slightly. Taste, and adjust the seasoning by adding more salt or lemon juice as required.

Either spoon the hummus into a bowl to serve or spread it directly onto your board. Either way, drizzle over some olive oil and scatter the pine nuts, sesame seeds and parsley over the top to finish.

ROASTED RAINBOW CRUDITÉS

These giant roasted vegetable dippers make a nice alternative to the usual raw crudités. I usually keep the stalks and roots on them for a more rustic vibe, and use whatever vegetables you fancy, either alongside or instead of my suggestions – cauliflower, fennel, asparagus all work well. You'll also see I roast these briefly at a very high heat, the aim being not to cook them but to add a little extra colour and flavour.

SERVES 6

4 long, thin carrots, peeled and quartered lengthways
12 spring onions/scallions, left whole
12 baby leeks, outer layer removed
150 g/5 oz. long French beans
3 Romano peppers, quartered lengthwise and deseeded
6 long broccolini, left whole
a bunch of large radishes
3 tablespoons olive oil
sea salt flakes and freshly ground black pepper

Preheat the oven to 240°C (475°F) Gas 9.

Place all the vegetables onto a large roasting pan being careful not to overcrowd them. Drizzle with the olive oil and season generously with salt and pepper.

Roast in the preheated oven for 8–10 minutes, then remove the pan from the oven – the vegetables should still have some crunch and not be too floppy.

To serve, pile them high on your board with a dip close by.

BLUSHING PICKLE

A decent pickle is something everyone should have in their repertoire. This medley of sharp red onions and crunchy radishes will go with pretty much everything on your vegan garden board.

MAKES A 500-ML/2-CUP JAR

2 red onions, sliced into fine rings
200 g/7 oz. radishes, thinly sliced
1 teaspoon fennel seeds
1 teaspoon pink peppercorns
1 teaspoon coriander seeds
2 tablespoons caster/granulated sugar
1 teaspoon rock salt
375 ml/1½ cups apple cider vinegar

a 500-ml/2-cup capacity sterilized jar

Put the sliced onions in a heatproof bowl and cover with boiling water. Leave them to blanch for 1 minute, then tip into a colander and rinse under cold running water, shaking off the excess water. Return the onions to the bowl, add the radishes and mix together. Transfer the vegetables to the sterilized jar.

Put all the remaining ingredients in a saucepan with 60 ml/¼ cup water and set over a high heat. As soon as the liquid starts to bubble and the sugar has dissolved, remove from the heat and pour into the jar. Leave to cool before eating.

CUCUMBER PICKLE

This delicious, slightly Asian-inspired cucumber pickle adds a nice tang to most meals with a subtle heat coming from the dried chilli/chile. This goes really well with my No Bird Chicken Pies (page 58).

MAKES A 500-ML/2-CUP JAR

1 cucumber (about 350 g/12 oz.)
3 tablespoons rock salt
a few sprigs of dill, left whole
250 ml/1 cup rice vinegar (or white distilled vinegar)

½ tablespoon fennel seeds
1 dried chilli/chile pepper (whole)
pinch of sesame seeds
2 tablespoons caster/granulated sugar

a 500-ml/2-cup capacity sterilized jar

Halve the cucumber lengthways and run a teaspoon down the middle to remove some of the seeds and watery centre.

Slice the cucumber into chunky crescents, combine with the rock salt and leave to rest in a sieve/strainer for about 30–60 minutes. Discard the excess water, give the cucumber a good rinse under cold running water, pat dry with paper towels and transfer to the sterilized jar along with the sprigs of dill.

Put all the remaining ingredients together in a saucepan set over a high heat. As soon as it starts to bubble and the sugar has dissolved, remove from the heat and pour into the jar. Leave to cool before eating.

EDIBLE FLOWER POTS

I created these conversation-starting edible flower pots for a large event when I wanted something that looked beautiful but that was still substantial to eat. The idea is you're eating through the layers you would find in any flower bed. At the bottom you have the potato 'rocks', then bean 'gravel', hummus 'mud', olive 'soil' and finally the flowers. The hummus is loosely based on a falafel mixture, with herbs giving it both the necessary green hue and plenty of fresh flavour. Ground dehydrated olives work perfectly as the top layer of soil and I like to use bright little violas or pansies for the contrast against it.

MAKES 6 INDIVIDUAL SERVINGS

SOIL (GROUND DRIED OLIVES)
450 g/1 lb. pitted black olives (start making this the day before)

ROCKS (ROASTED NEW POTATOES)
a small bunch of fresh rosemary or sage
600 g/1 lb. 5 oz. baby new potatoes
olive oil, for drizzling
salt and freshly ground black pepper

GRAVEL (BEAN AND LENTIL SALAD)
400-g/14-oz. can mixed beans or black-eyed beans (240 g/8½ oz. drained weight)
240 g/8½ oz. pre-cooked green or Puy lentils
30 g/¼ cup finely chopped red onion
a small handful each of freshly chopped coriander/cilantro, flat-leaf parsley and mint
3 tablespoons olive oil
3 tablespoons apple cider vinegar
salt and freshly ground black pepper

MUD (HERBY HUMMUS)
1 teaspoon coriander seeds
1 teaspoon cumin seeds
400-g/14-oz. can chickpeas/garbanzo beans, drained
a handful of fresh coriander/cilantro
a small bunch of flat-leaf parsley
1 garlic clove, peeled
1 tablespoon finely chopped red onion
a small squeeze of fresh lemon juice
salt and freshly ground black pepper
olive oil, for drizzling

TO ASSEMBLE AND FINISH
100 g/4 oz. salad leaves, shredded, dressed with lemon juice and seasoned
6 baby carrots or radishes, with leaves (optional)
rocket/arugula leaves or chives
1 punnet edible flowers, such as violas

a baking sheet, lined with baking parchment
6 x 7.5-cm/3-inch diameter terracotta plant pots (ideally glazed)

Start with making the dried soil as it takes a day in the oven to dehydrate. Preheat the oven to 90°C (190°F) Gas ¼. Rinse the olives and shake off as much water as possible (draining them on paper towels helps remove more moisture from them). Place the olives on the lined baking sheet, pop it into the preheated oven for about 8 hours or until the olives are brittle and hard to the touch. Leave to cool for 30 minutes, then pulse in a food processor (not a blender, it will turn them into a paste), until you have a fine grained olive crumb. Store in an airtight container until needed.

To make the potato 'rocks', preheat the oven to 200°C (400°F) Gas 6.

Strip the rosemary needles, or sage leaves, from their stalks and finely chop them. Drizzle olive oil over the potatoes in a roasting pan, season generously and fold in the rosemary or sage. Roast in the preheated oven for about 30 minutes, or until they are fork-tender.

To make the bean and lentil 'gravel', drain and rinse the beans and lentils, then add to a mixing bowl with the red onion and fold in all the herbs. Pour over the olive oil and vinegar, season generously and stir to mix.

To make the herby hummus 'mud', dry-fry the coriander and cumin seeds for a minute, or until you start to smell their aroma as that tells you they are ready. Tip them into a food processor along with the rest of the 'mud' ingredients (except the oil) and pulse until you have a smooth paste. Add a splash of water to loosen the mixture if necessary. Taste and add more salt or lemon juice as required.

To assemble the pots, slice one of the cooked potatoes into rounds to cover the hole at the bottom of each pot, this is to help stop any juices leaking out then add a few more of the roasted potatoes to the bottom of each one, just enough to create your first layer.

Into each pot, spoon over a couple of tablespoons of the bean and lentil salad and gently flatten and level with the back of a spoon. Add a pinch or two of the dressed salad leaves and pat down before spooning over the hummus, about a tablespoon or just enough to cover the top. Again, use the back of a spoon to smooth and level the surface. (Now is a good time to clean the inside edge of the pots by giving each one a quick wipe with paper towels.)

Next, gently scatter some dried olive crumb over the top of the hummus, ensuring the entire surface is covered – you don't want it too deep, just enough to cover. Finally, 'plant' your radish or carrot in the top of each (if using), stick some rocket/arugula or chives in next to each other along the edge of each pot and 'plant' a few edible flowers in each one to finish.

NO-BIRD CHICKEN PIES

My moreish vegan pies are delicious, comforting and hugely popular with everyone. They are made using canned jackfruit (now widely available), which, once cooked in a savoury sauce, transforms into a meat-free filling with a good texture and real depth of flavour.

MAKES 4 INDIVIDUAL PIES

565-g/20-oz. can jackfruit in brine, drained (280 g/10 oz. drained weight)
1 white onion, diced
2 garlic cloves, sliced
130 g/1 cup canned chickpeas/garbanzo beans, drained and rinsed
570 ml/2½ scant cups vegetable stock
1 teaspoon Marmite/yeast extract
1 tablespoon cornflour/cornstarch
2 tablespoons freshly chopped flat-leaf parsley
1 tablespoon dried oregano
a squeeze of fresh lemon juice
500 g/1 lb. 2 oz. ready-made vegan shortcrust pastry
salt and freshly ground black pepper
olive oil, for frying

4 x 7.5 cm/3-inch diameter mini pudding moulds, greased

You can either make the jackfruit filling the day before or just before you are ready to make your pies.

Drain and rinse the jackfruit, then pat it dry with paper towels. Slice it into small bite-sized chunks. Heat a splash of olive oil in a frying pan/skillet and fry the jackfruit for about 6 minutes, until it starts to colour. Once done, remove it from the pan and set aside until needed.

Add more olive oil to the pan if needed and fry the onion for 5 minutes until translucent, then add the garlic and chickpeas/garbanzo beans and reintroduce the jackfruit.

Add the stock and Marmite/yeast extract, and season with salt and pepper. Cover the pan and simmer for about 5 minutes, then remove the lid and simmer until the stock has reduced by three-quarters, this should take about 15 minutes. Add more stock and continue cooking if the jackfruit hasn't softened fully.

Make a slurry with the cornflour/cornstarch, and 1 tablespoon water and pour it into the pan, stirring to ensure it is well incorporated, it should thicken the sauce immediately. You want a nice coating of liquid in the filling but not so much that it is sloppy. Finally, remove from the heat, fold in the parsley and oregano and add a little squeeze of lemon juice. Cover and set aside.

Preheat the oven to 180°C (350°F) Gas 4.

Cut the pastry into five equal portions, wrap one of the portions in clingfilm/plastic wrap and reserve for later. Roll the remaining four portions into balls, then roll out into thin rounds, each about 3 mm/^{1}/8 inch thick. Line each greased pudding mould with a pastry round, trimming off any excess with a sharp knife. For each pie, crumple a piece of baking parchment to loosen it then stretch it back out and carefully place inside the pudding mould, on top of the pastry. Fill with baking beans and blind bake in the preheated oven for 20 minutes.

Once done, remove the beans and baking paper, fill each pudding mould with the jackfruit filling all the way to the top. Divide the reserved piece of pastry into four pieces. Roll these out to make lids for your pies, and using a wet finger, dampen the rim of the pastry lids and place them on top, pinching a little to keep them in place. Pop back in the oven to bake for about 15 minutes, or until the top pastry piece on each pie is golden and cooked.

Leave the pies to cool a little before serving as the filling will be very hot. Serve with my Cucumber Pickle (page 53), if you fancy it.

BANANA BLOSSOM TEMPURA

The banana blossom is the flower of the banana tree and makes an unusual and tasty vegan bite. It has a mild flavour and a beautiful smooth texture. As I don't live near any banana trees (turns out they are sparse in Hertfordshire...). I get mine online in canned form. Once rinsed and dressed in a light, super-crispy tempura batter, the blossoms are delicious served with a tangy and chunky tomato salsa.

SERVES 4

100 g/1 cup cornflour/cornstarch
70 g/½ cup plain/all-purpose flour, plus extra for dusting
2 tablespoons freshly chopped dill
250 ml/1 cup soda water
260 g/9 oz. canned banana blossoms (drained weight)
about 500 ml/2 cups vegetable oil, for deep-frying
salt and freshly ground black pepper

SHARP TOMATO SALSA

3 tablespoons chopped cherry tomatoes
1 tablespoon finely diced red onion
1 small fresh green chilli/chile, deseeded and sliced
3 tablespoons freshly chopped flat-leaf parsley
2 tablespoons olive oil
1 tablespoon malt vinegar
freshly squeezed lemon juice, to taste

First make the tomato salsa. Simply combine all of the ingredients in a small bowl and season to taste with lemon juice. Chill until ready to serve.

Next make the tempura batter. Put the cornflour/cornstarch, flour and dill in a mixing bowl and season well with salt and pepper. Pour in the soda water and whisk with a fork (don't be tempted to over-whisk, a few lumps are okay).

Pour the vegetable oil into a large saucepan and set over a medium heat. Drain the banana blossoms, rinse them under running water and shake of the excess. Cut them into quarters lengthways (if they are already halved, then just halve them again). Dust the banana blossoms in a little plain/all-purpose flour then, holding them in tongs, dip them into the tempura batter. Lift them out and let some of the excess batter drip off before carefully dropping them into the hot oil to deep-fry for about 4 minutes, or until the batter is crisp (this batter won't go golden). Once crispy, drain the banana blossoms on paper towels before placing them on your board. Season and serve with the sharp tomato salsa.

PICNIC

VILLAGE-STYLE ARTICHOKE BULBS

This simple dish always reminds me of being with my family in my Cypriot grandmother's kitchen in north London. Just hanging around there waiting for dinner to cook while picking leaves from an artichoke, dipping them in a little vinaigrette and stripping the flesh off with my teeth. Once all the leaves had gone, we'd cut away the feathery centre from the artichoke heart and thinly slice it; and it's that last bit we'd all fight over!

MAKES 2 BULBS, TO SHARE

2 large fresh artichoke bulbs, stalks
   at the base trimmed
6 fresh lemon slices
salt, to taste

VINAIGRETTE
6 tablespoons olive oil
6 tablespoons apple cider vinegar
1 tablespoon English mustard
salt and freshly ground black pepper

Fill a large saucepan with water and set it over a medium heat to bring it to the boil. Add a few pinches of salt and the lemon slices.

Once simmering, add the prepared artichoke bulbs to the pan and cook for about 15 minutes. Remove them from the water, put them upside-down on a plate and let them steam dry.

I like to make my vinaigrette by simply adding the olive oil, vinegar, mustard and a pinch each of salt and pepper to a screwtop jar and giving it a good shake to emulsify. Alternatively, put all the ingredients in a small bowl and whisk with a fork until combined and emulsified.

Serve the artichoke bulbs as they come – letting people pull a leaf off the artichoke, dip the stalk end into the vinaigrette and then strip the little morsel of flesh off the leaf with their teeth.

GREEK-STYLE SCOTCH EGGS WITH ROMESCO SAUCE

A homemade Scotch egg is a wonderful thing and these are inspired by a Greek delicacy, koupes. I lace the meat with warming cinnamon, cumin, nutmeg and a little lemon zest to keep things vibrant, and instead of breadcrumbs they have a crunchy bulgur wheat coating. For me, a rich variation on a Romesco sauce is the go-to condiment – slather it over the eggs or halve them and use it as a dip.

MAKES 6

7 eggs
170 g/1 cup fine grain bulgur wheat
a pinch of ground turmeric
450 g/1 lb. good-quality pork sausages
½ teaspoon ground cumin
½ tablespoon ground cinnamon
freshly grated nutmeg, to taste
a handful each of freshly chopped
  flat-leaf parsley and coriander/cilantro
grated zest of 1 lemon
about 260 g/2 cups plain/all-purpose
  flour, plus extra for dusting
2 tablespoons mild chilli/chili powder
salt and freshly ground black pepper
500 ml/2 cups vegetable oil, for
  deep-frying

ROMESCO SAUCE
1 slice of white bread
1 garlic clove
50 g/generous ⅓ cup walnuts
80 ml/⅓ cup olive oil
100 g/3½ oz. roasted red (bell) peppers
  from a jar
25 g/1 oz. sun-dried tomatoes
a pinch of sugar
1 tablespoon tomato purée/paste
a generous pinch of smoked paprika
2 tablespoons freshly chopped flat-leaf
  parsley, plus extra to garnish
salt and freshly ground black pepper

First make the Romesco Sauce. Preheat the oven to 180°C (350°F) Gas 4.

Put the bread, garlic (still with the skin on, left whole) and the walnuts onto a baking sheet and bake in the preheated oven for about 8–10 minutes. If the walnuts still have some skin on, I gently rub them all together in my hands and you'll find most flakes off, but don't worry about getting it all off. Pour two thirds of the olive oil into a food processor along with all the other ingredients, making sure you peel the garlic and trim the stalk end off. Pulse to a fairly fine consistency or to your preference, taste for seasoning and then fold through the remaining olive oil. Cover and chill until ready to serve.

To make the Scotch eggs, put six of the eggs in a saucepan with cold water to cover and bring to the boil, then reduce the heat and simmer for 4 minutes. Transfer the eggs to a bowl of cold water and once cooled, peel them. Set aside until needed.

Put the bulgur and turmeric in a large heatproof bowl and pour in 250 ml/1 cup boiling water. (The turmeric is just to colour the bulgur rather than to add taste, so remember a little goes a long way.) Cover and leave to hydrate for 20 minutes. Once hydrated, tip the bulgur onto a plate and leave it to air dry for a further 30 minutes.

Snip the ends off the sausages and squeeze the meat out of the casings and into a large mixing bowl. Add the cumin, cinnamon, nutmeg, herbs and lemon zest and season generously with salt and pepper. Mix well to combine everything.

When you are ready to assemble your Scotch eggs, get everything out in front of you. Whisk the remaining egg in a bowl and place it next to a bowl containing the flour and chilli/chili powder mixed together. Divide the sausage meat mixture into six equal portions. Dust the cooked eggs in flour. (Dust your hands in flour to make handling the sticky sausage meat easier.) Flatten one portion of the sausage meat into a flat round about 1 cm/³⁄8 inch thick, place a flour-dusted egg in the centre and fold the sausage meat around the egg, massaging it into place until the egg is fully sealed. If the sausage meat starts to stick to your hands, dust them again.

Roll the sausage meat-coated egg in the flour, then the egg, then into the bulgur. Cradle the Scotch egg in your hands to press the bulgur into the sausage meat and set aside. Repeat until you have six Scotch eggs ready to cook.

Pour the vegetable oil into a deep-sided saucepan and set it over a medium heat. The oil is hot enough when a pinch of bulgur dropped into it sizzles immediately.

It's best to cook the eggs in batches, being careful not to overcrowd the pan. To do this, put a Scotch egg on a slotted spoon and carefully lower it into the hot oil. Leave it to cook for a few minutes before gently turning it over in the oil if not fully submerged. After about 6–7 minutes it will be golden and cooked. Remove with the slotted spoon and place on paper towels to drain. Let the Scotch eggs rest for 10 minutes before serving, with the Romesco Sauce on the side or as a dip.

PIMM'S SUMMER SALAD

Quintessentially British, drinking a glass of Pimm's tells me it's
the start of summer. A chilled gulp full of crunchy cucumber and fresh
mint... the tangy bite of a strawberry... just perfect. My Pimm's summer
salad is inspired by memories of half-cut summer days and losing
money on misguided bets at the Royal Ascot race meetings...

SERVES 6

1½ punnets large strawberries
    (about 36), hulled and quartered
3 large cucumbers
about 120 g/4 oz. watercress
    (a large handful)
1 small red onion, very thinly sliced
leaves from about 12 sprigs of fresh
    mint, torn
a large handful of toasted walnuts
    (optional)

PIMM'S DRESSING
6 tablespoons Pimm's No1 Cup
3 tablespoons olive oil
3 teaspoons freshly squeezed lemon
    juice
3 teaspoons white balsamic vinegar
grated zest of 1½ oranges
salt and freshly ground black pepper

Hull and quarter the strawberries. Cut the cucumber in half lengthways. Use
a spoon to scrap the watery seeds out of the centre and discard. Slice the flesh
into thin crescents about 1 cm/3/8 inch thick.

Put all of the dressing ingredients in a large bowl. Whisk with a fork until
combined and emulsified. Season to taste with salt and pepper.

Add the prepared strawberries and cucumber to the bowl, along with the
watercress, sliced onion and torn mint. Gently fold all the ingredients together to
ensure the salad is well coated, then transfer to your picnic board or into a clean
serving bowl, as preferred.

If it takes your fancy, a large handful of toasted walnuts adds a nice crunch,
so scatter these over the finished salad, if using.

BURNT-BUTTER POTTED SHRIMPS & CRAB

Here, a deliciously nutty burnt butter with just a hint of spicy heat and pockets of crushed coriander seeds, encases the sweet crab and shrimps. It's best served at room temperature with a cold glass of sauvignon blanc. The herby melba toasts make the ideal partner.

MAKES 4 SERVINGS

100 g/7 tablespoons butter
2 small pinches of saffron threads
2 teaspoons coriander seeds, lightly cracked
1 whole dried red chilli/chile
70 g/2½ oz. cooked and peeled brown shrimp

1 tablespoon freshly chopped flat-leaf parsley
grated zest of ¾ lemon
100 g/3½ oz. crab meat (mixed white and brown)
salt and freshly ground black pepper

a 300-ml/10 oz. capacity Kilner jar or 4 x 75-ml/3 oz. individual ramekins

Put the butter, half the saffron threads, half the coriander seeds and the whole dried chilli/chile in a small saucepan. Bring to a simmer and cook for 5–6 minutes until the butter foams and starts to turn brown, then immediately remove the pan from the heat. Once the butter stops foaming and settles, carefully pour the golden clarified butter into a clean bowl along with the chilli/chile and as many coriander seeds as possible.

Give the pan a quick wipe, then return about half the clarified butter to the pan along with the shrimps and remaining saffron threads and coriander seeds. Warm this through for 30 seconds.

In a separate bowl, very gently fold together the chopped parsley and lemon zest with the white and brown crab meat, then season very generously with salt and pepper. Use a light hand when folding it together as it should stay coarse.

Pour the shrimps with any butter from the saucepan into the crab mixture and again, very gently fold together. Decant this into a clean Kilner jar (or four ramekins), level the top of the mixture with the back of a spoon and chill in the fridge for 30 minutes to set.

Once set, spoon the remaining melted butter over the top and chill again. To serve, remove from the fridge at least 30 minutes beforehand and serve with crisp melba toasts (see recipe opposite).

HERBY MELBA TOASTS

Melba toast is a great friend to most dips and ideal to have floating around on your picnic board. It's incredibly easy to make and I like to incorporate some herbs into the toast – my favourite is thyme.

MAKES 12

4 thin slices of soft white bread

1 tablespoon dried herbs of your choice, such as thyme, sage or rosemary, as preferred

Preheat the oven to 180°C (350°F) Gas 4.

Trim the crusts from the slices of bread, scatter a small amount of dried herbs over each slice then use a rolling pin to roll the bread as flat as you can get it. Trim the edges and cut into fingers – I aim to get about 3–4 toasts per slice of bread.

Place on a baking sheet and bake in the preheated oven for 15–20 minutes until they just start to take on some colour. Remove from the oven and cool.

Store in an airtight container until ready to use. Perfect served with the Burnt-butter Potted Shrimps and Crab (see opposite), dips or cheese.

CROWNED SPINACH & FETA QUICHE

A quiche is one of my ultimate summertime foods and I like to bake the pastry base in a cake pan with high sides so that once it's cooked it has a 'crown' around the crust. Try this delicious combination of salty sharp feta, earthy spinach and punchy oven-roasted tomatoes.

SERVES 6

125 g/¾ cup mixed baby tomatoes
180 g/6½ oz. ready-rolled shortcrust
 pastry
plain/all-purpose flour, for dusting
4 eggs, plus 1 egg for egg wash
90 g/3 oz. smoked bacon lardons
100 g/3½ oz. fresh baby spinach leaves
125 ml/½ cup double/heavy cream

125 ml/½ cup full-fat/whole milk
70 g/¾ cup grated mature/sharp
 Cheddar
a generous pinch of freshly grated
 nutmeg
100 g/3½ oz. feta
salt and freshly ground black pepper

olive oil, for shallow-frying

a 23-cm/9-inch round cake pan, buttered

Preheat the oven to 200°C (400°F) Gas 6.

Halve the tomatoes and place them on a baking sheet. Season with salt and pepper and cook in the preheated oven for about 10 minutes, or until they have softened, then turn the oven down to 180°C (350°F) Gas 4.

Roll out the pastry on a flour-dusted surface until 3 mm/⅛ inch thick and use to line the prepared cake pan. Trim off the excess pastry at the very top of the cake pan. Prick all over the base with a fork and bake in the preheated oven for 20 minutes. After 20 minutes, brush the pastry with egg wash and return to the oven to bake for a further 6 minutes.

While the pastry case/shell is cooking, you can make the filling. Put the bacon lardons in a frying pan/skillet with a little olive oil and fry until crispy. Pour away the excess oil, turn off the heat and drop the spinach into the pan to wilt in the residual heat.

Put the eggs, cream and milk in a bowl and beat together. Stir in the Cheddar cheese, roasted tomatoes, browned lardons and wilted spinach and season generously with salt, pepper and the nutmeg, to taste.

Pour the mixture into the blind-baked pastry case, it should only fill it halfway up, crumble the feta in chunks over the top and then bake in the still-hot oven for 25–30 minutes, or until it has the slightest wobble. Leave to cool in the cake pan before removing to serve on your board.

LEMON & THYME CURD

I want a lemon curd that makes me pout, wince, and then soothes my palate with the aromatic scent of thyme and just enough sweetness to keep me going back for more. So I made this to satisfy that (very specific) craving.

MAKES A 300-ML/1¹/4 CUP JAR

4 egg yolks
150 g/³/4 cup white/granulated sugar
grated zest and freshly squeezed juice of 4 lemons
5 tablespoons cornflour/cornstarch
3 tablespoons cold water
30 g/2 tablespoons butter, softened
1 tablespoon fresh thyme leaves, plus extra to garnish

Whisk the egg yolks with the sugar in a bowl and, once combined, fold in the lemon zest and juice.

Combine the cornflour/cornstarch with the cold water together in a small bowl to make a slurry and then whisk into the egg mixture. Whisk the softened butter into the egg mixture.

Pour the mixture into a saucepan set over a low heat and add the thyme leaves. Bring to a gentle simmer, whisking continuously. As soon as it starts to bubble and transforms into a nice glossy curd, remove from the heat.

Decant into a clean jar, cover and cool before serving on your picnic board with the chamomile shortbread.

CHAMOMILE SHORTBREAD

What says picnic more than shortbread (besides, perhaps wasps)? This recipe includes crushed dried chamomile to give it a floral note that works well with my Lemon and Thyme Curd (opposite). If you can't source the flowers, crack open a few pure chamomile teabags.

MAKES 24 FINGERS

120 g/1 stick butter, softened
a pinch of salt
50 g/¹/4 cup caster/granulated sugar
50 g/¹/2 cup cornflour/cornstarch
150 g/1 generous cup plain/all-purpose flour
1 tablespoon finely ground chamomile flowers and leaves

Preheat the oven to 170°C (340°F) Gas 3.

Cream the butter, sugar and salt together in a bowl with a hand-held electric whisk. Sift the cornflour/cornstarch and flour into the creamed butter mix, along with the chamomile, and beat until combined.

Tip this scraggy mess out onto a clean surface and knead together until it forms a dough; it will be drier than a regular shortbread dough. Place this in between two sheets of baking parchment and push it down flat with your hands. Roll out, still between the baking parchment sheets, until it is about 1 cm/³/8 inch thick.

Cut the shortbread into fingers about 7.5 x 2.5 cm/ 3 x 1 inches in size and carefully (I use a palette knife) place them on a non-stick baking sheet. Bake in the preheated oven for 15 minutes.

Remove and, using the palette knife again, place the cooked shortbread on a wire rack to cool. Once cooled, store in an airtight container until ready to serve.

GROWN-UP SUMMER BERRY TERRINE

This was one of my childhood favourites, but I now like a more adult version with a little shot of Chambord in the mix. It's all in the name; the ultimate dessert for a summer picnic.

SERVES 6

300 g/3 cups strawberries, plus extra
   to decorate
350 g/2½ cups raspberries, plus extra
   to decorate
150 g/generous 1 cup blackberries, plus
   extra to decorate
100 g/½ cup blueberries, plus extra
   to garnish

100 g/½ cup caster/granulated sugar
2 tablespoons Chambord (or other red
   berry-flavoured liqueur)
400 g/14 oz. good-quality white bread
a few sprigs of fresh lemon thyme or
   mint leaves, to garnish
Vanilla Cream (see page 146), to serve
   (optional)

900-g/2-lb loaf pan

Hull and quarter the strawberries and put them in a saucepan with the other berries, sugar, Chambord and 1 tablespoon water. Heat gently for a few minutes to soften the berries and to release their juices, then set aside.

Double-line the loaf pan with two sheets of clingfilm/plastic wrap, overhanging by a few inches each side.

Slice the white bread into 1-cm/³/8-inch slices, removing the crusts. Cut some of the slices into shape to fit snugly along the bottom of the lined loaf pan. Spoon in half the berry mixture and a third of the juice.

Line the top of the berries with another layer of snug-fitting bread (cut into shape) and top with the remaining half of berries and half the remaining juice. Finally, lay the final layer of bread on top, pushing it down a little and then pour over the remaining juice.

Fold over the clingfilm/plastic wrap, push down a little to flatten and then rest in the fridge for a couple of hours or ideally overnight. Place a heavy weight on top (a can of soup, pint of milk, etc.) while resting in the fridge.

To serve, simply tip out of the loaf pan, unwrap the clingfilm/plastic wrap and decorate with the extra uncooked berries over the top, dotted with lemon thyme sprigs or mint leaves.

Serve with a bowl of vanilla cream for dolloping, if liked.

OCEAN

VIETNAMESE CHARRED SQUID NOODLE SALAD

My recipe for squid salad takes its lead from Vietnamese flavours. It's fresh, zingy and bright with plenty of lime juice, fish sauce and slices of hot bird's eye chilli/chile. If you're not keen on intense heat you can swap the bird's eye for a milder variety. This is great as a stand alone plate but also weaves into the Ocean board as a nice taste contrast.

SERVES 6 TO SHARE, 2 AS A MAIN

1 tablespoon sesame seeds
60 g/2–3 oz. dried vermicelli rice noodles
1 teaspoon sesame oil
50 g/½ cup mangetouts/snow peas
½ cucumber
2 spring onions/scallions
100 g/3½ oz. baby spinach leaves
a handful of fresh coriander/cilantro
a handful of fresh mint leaves
400 g/14 oz. raw squid tubes, cleaned
salt, to season
olive oil, to drizzle

VIETNAMESE DRESSING

5-cm/2-inch piece of root ginger, grated
2 tablespoons fish sauce
2 tablespoons freshly squeezed lime juice
1 garlic clove, crushed
1 tablespoon clear runny honey
a pinch of salt
1 tablespoon sesame oil
1 fresh red bird's eye chilli/chile, plus extra to garnish, or a milder variety if preferred

First, make the dressing. Combine all the ingredients (except the bird's eye chilli/chile) in a small bowl and whisk with a fork to combine. Thinly slice the chilli/chile, reserving a few slivers to garnish, and add to the dressing. Next, toast the sesame seeds in a dry frying pan/skillet. Set both aside until needed.

Put the noodles in a heatproof bowl and pour in boiling water to cover. Leave until hydrated (or follow the specific instructions on your packet). Tip them into a sieve/strainer set over a bowl, toss with the sesame oil to stop them sticking together and leave to drain further – you want them as dry as possible.

Put the mangetouts/snow peas in a heatproof bowl and pour over boiling water to cover. Blanch for 1 minute, then drain and plunge into a bowl of iced water to cool. Drain again and put in a large bowl. Halve the cucumber lengthways and use a spoon to scoop out the watery seeds. Cut into slices about 3 mm/$\frac{1}{8}$ inch thick and at an angle. Drop these into the bowl. Trim and thinly slice the spring onions/scallions and add these to the bowl. Finally, add the spinach and rip the herbs straight in. Spoon in two-thirds of the dressing, toss everything together and leave the salad to soak up the dressing.

Prepare the squid by placing the back of a spoon inside each squid tube, then slice the top of the squid widthways (the spoon will stop you slicing all the way through the squid and cutting it into rings). Drizzle with a little olive oil and season with a pinch of salt.

Heat a griddle/grill pan until smoking. Add the prepared squid tubes and cook for 1–2 minutes, or until the flesh turns opaque and charred lines appear, then turn over and cook the other side in the same way.

When you are ready to serve, lift the noodle salad out of the bowl, shaking off any excess dressing and place it directly onto your board. Arrange the charred squid on top, pour over the remaining salad dressing and garnish with the reserved slivers of red chilli/chile and a sprinkling of the toasted sesame seeds.

FENNEL & GREEN APPLE SALAD

This is a refreshing salad that works really well on my ocean-themed board. The aniseedy notes of the fennel and the tarragon complement the seafood dishes on offer and the apples add a crisp sharpness. I quite like the heat that the green chilli/chile brings to the dish, but it's an optional extra. Serve this chilled, straight from the fridge.

SERVES 4 TO SHARE

1 fennel bulb
freshly squeezed juice of 1 lime
1 tart, crisp green eating apple, such as
   a Granny Smith

¼ cucumber
½ fresh green chilli/chile (optional)
a small handful of fresh mint leaves
leaves from a sprig of fresh tarragon
1 tablespoon olive oil
a pinch of salt

Thinly slice the fennel bulb and chop the fronds. Put it in a large bowl and pour over the freshly squeezed lime juice.

Leave the peel on the apple. Core it, slice in half and cut into thin slices about 3 mm/⅛ inch thick. Add to the fennel in the bowl and toss everything in the lime juice as it will help to prevent the apple slices from browning.

Quarter the cucumber lengthways, use a spoon to scoop out the watery seeds and then thinly slice to about the same thickness as the apple and add it to the bowl with the fennel and apple.

Deseed the green chilli/chile (if using), slice very thinly and add to the bowl.

Finally, rip the mint and tarragon straight into the bowl. (Go easy on the tarragon as it does have quite a strong flavour.)

Drizzle over the olive oil and add the pinch of salt. Toss everything together once last time and chill in the fridge until ready to serve, but try to prepare it no more than 30 minutes before serving, to keep everything nice and crisp.

BAKED SCALLOPS IN CHIPOTLE BUTTER

Nature provided these perfectly formed bites in their own serving plates so grazers can grab one, scoff it down and move on! I'm a big fan of the scallop and this simple recipe ensures that they stay the star of the show, with the chipotle butter playing a winning supporting role.

MAKES 6

6 fresh scallops in the half shell,
   including the roe
40 g/3 tablespoons butter, softened
1 garlic clove, crushed
½ teaspoon chipotle chilli/chile flakes
½ teaspoon salt
½ tablespoon freshly chopped coriander/
   cilantro
bread, to serve (optional)
1 lemon, cut into 6 wedges, to serve

Preheat the oven to 230°C (450°F) Gas 8.

Prepare the scallops by removing the tough little hinge that attaches the scallop to the shell and any membrane surrounding the scallop. Rinse the scallops under running water, pat them dry with paper towels and set aside until needed. Rinse and dry the shells.

To make the chipotle butter, put the softened butter, crushed garlic, chipotle flakes, salt and coriander/cilantro into a small bowl. Whip together with a spoon until well combined.

Dab a small amount of chipotle butter in the base of each shell, place the scallops and roe on top and then put another dot of butter on top of each one. Don't be afraid to use all the chipotle butter!

Transfer the shells to a baking sheet and cook in the preheated oven for 4–5 minutes. Remove from the oven and serve with bread for dipping in the melted butter (if you fancy it) and lemon wedges for squeezing.

Note: You can also cook these on the barbecue/outdoor grill by placing the shells straight onto the grill and just turning the scallops over in their shells after a few minutes of cooking.

BAKED LANGOUSTINES WITH BLACK GARLIC BUTTER

Langoustines are delicious. They only take about 6 minutes to cook and reward you with sweet and succulent meat that is perfect with a chilled glass of dry white wine. I serve mine with a black garlic butter and, when in season, a handful of finely chopped wild garlic/ramps.

SERVES 6

12 whole, fresh langoustines (or large shell-on prawns/shrimp)
3 black garlic cloves, peeled
120 g/1 stick butter, softened
3 tablespoons finely chopped wild garlic leaves/ramps (or flat-leaf parsley),
plus extra to garnish
a squeeze of fresh lemon juice
salt, to taste
olive oil, for drizzling
½ tablespoon finely chopped fresh red chilli/chile, to garnish
some good bread, to serve

Preheat the oven to 200°C (400°F) Gas 6.

To prepare the langoustines, turn them on their back and, using a sharp, heavy knife, halve them lengthways (you'll see a natural line in between the legs). Remove the waist tract if you can and, with a teaspoon, scoop out the brown meat from the head. Keep them in the fridge until ready to use.

Mash the black garlic using a pestle and mortar with a generous pinch of salt until you have a paste – I quite like to leave a few lumps in mine. Put the softened butter in a small bowl and cream with a spoon. Add the black garlic paste and mix together to combine. Follow with the chopped wild garlic leaves/ramps.

Drizzle a little olive oil into a roasting pan and lay the langoustines in shell-side down – don't overcrowd them. Dot each langoustine tail with black garlic butter and keep going until you have used it all (I do this in the knowledge that I'll be wiping the excess melted butter onto a lump of bread and sticking it in my mouth before anyone else gets a look in). Pop in the preheated oven for about 6 minutes, or until the flesh is opaque and the shells have taken on a redder hue.

Transfer the langoustines to your board, pour over any melted butter and juices from the pan, scatter the chopped red chilli/chile and wild garlic/ramps over the top and finish with a squeeze of lemon juice and salt. Serve with bread.

LOBSTER TAILS WITH JALAPEÑO & TOMATO

Lobster tails are a real luxury, but when you do want to splurge out on a foodie treat, this is the way to go. The jalapeño marinade adds a fiery kick whilst still keeping the lobster moist. Once I've placed the lobster tails on the board, I always drizzle a little more of the leftover juice over the top; it's great for dipping bread into. Just saying...

SERVES 6

2 fresh red jalapeño chillies/chiles, sliced
1 large garlic clove, crushed
1 tablespoon freshly squeezed lemon
 juice, plus extra to serve
60 ml/¼ cup olive oil
2 tablespoons tomato purée/paste
a pinch of sugar
2 tablespoons freshly chopped coriander/
 cilantro
6 lobster tails (100 g/3½ oz. each)
½ teaspoon sea salt
some good bread, to serve

Preheat the oven to 200°C (400°F) Gas 6.

Put the chillies/chiles and garlic in a pestle and mortar and grind to a paste. Add the lemon juice, olive oil and tomato purée/paste and mix to blend, then stir in the sugar and chopped coriander/cilantro to create a paste.

To prepare the lobster tails, use a sharp knife or kitchen scissors and cut the top of each lobster tail open along the centre but stop just before you reach the end, the point where it fans out. Use your fingers to prise open the shell and dislodge the lobster meat a bit, cracking it open further. Watch out for little pieces of shell clinging to the meat.

Place the tails on a baking sheet. Spoon an equal amount of the jalapeño and tomato paste onto each of the lobster tails and spread it over with the back of the spoon. Roast them in the preheated oven for about 10–12 minutes, or until the lobster flesh is cooked. (If your lobster tails are much bigger, it will take a little longer, but try to cook them for no more than 15 minutes otherwise the meat will become rubbery in texture.)

Add a squeeze of lemon juice and a sprinkling of salt just before serving with some good bread for dunking in the spicy juices. The fiery heat here works well with the cool crispness of the Fennel and Green Apple Salad (page 82).

STEAMED RAZOR CLAMS WITH GARLIC BUTTER

Razor clams are interesting... their white flesh actually resembles squid more than their closer cousins clams and mussels. They take only a few minutes to cook and all they need is a splash of white wine and a little seasoning to make them taste seriously good. They are great to share, and don't forget the bread for dunking in the delicious liquor!

SERVES 6

500 g/1 lb. 2 oz. razor clams, cleaned
60 ml/¼ cup olive oil
3 garlic cloves, sliced
a splash of white wine
30 g/2 tablespoons butter

a handful of freshly chopped
  flat-leaf parsley
a pinch of dried chilli/hot red pepper
  flakes
freshly squeezed juice of ¼ lemon
salt, to taste (optional)
some good bread, to serve

Rinse the razor clams well in cold, running water, discarding any that don't close properly when handled.

Heat the olive oil in a large lidded saucepan and drop in the garlic slices. Just before the garlic starts to brown, add the razor clams and give the pan a little shake. Pour in the wine, cover the pan with the lid and cook for just 2 minutes or so, until all the shells have opened and the meat has turned opaque.

Remove the lid, let the wine reduce for a further 1 minute, then drop in the butter and turn off the heat, swirling the pan gently to incorporate the butter.

Just before serving, throw in most of the parsley (holding a few pinches back to garnish) and chilli/hot red pepper flakes and squeeze in a little lemon juice. Taste one and if it needs salt (it doesn't usually, but always worth checking), sprinkle a little over the clams.

Pile the hot razor clams on your board or arrange them in a shallow dish or platter, drizzle over the sauce and sprinkle over the reserved chopped parsley. Serve with bread.

EAST END-STYLE VINEGARED MIXED SHELLFISH

I remember as a kid sitting with my dad in the local pub (as you did back then...) and there was always a fish stall outside. I'd be handed a polystyrene pot full of winkles, whelks and cockles splashed with some malt vinegar, and devoured the lot while my dad dived into a bowl of jellied eels. You can use already cooked and shelled seafood here if you prefer, more often than not I do, but here is the method for cooking them from fresh. You do need to wash and rinse them very thoroughly.

SERVES 6

140 g/1 cup fresh whelks, in their shells
140 g/1 cup fresh cockles, in their shells
50 g/2¾ cups raw unshelled prawns/
    shrimp
crushed ice, to serve

SPICY VINEGAR

250 ml/1 cup distilled malt vinegar
a pinch of sugar
1 teaspoon salt
1 bay leaf, fresh or dried
½ tablespoon black peppercorns
3 dried long red chillies/chiles

Wash the whelks thoroughly in several changes of water, then leave them to soak for 2 hours before cooking them in boiling salted water for about 12–15 minutes. Next, rinse the cockles under cold running water and discard any that are open. Soak them in salted water for 30 minutes before cooking them in boiling salted water for just 3–4 minutes, until all the shells open. Boil the prawns/shrimp in salted water for about 5 minutes, until they turn a vibrant pink. Drain. Spread all the cooked seafood out on a tray to cool and chill in the fridge until ready to serve.

Put the vinegar, sugar and salt in a small saucepan and bring it to a rapid boil. Once the sugar and salt have dissolved, turn off the heat and immediately drop in the bay leaf, black peppercorns and chillies/chiles. Leave to cool.

Serve the cooked, chilled shellfish in piles arranged on crushed ice on your board and liberally doused with the spicy vinegar. Happy days...

PICKLED SWORDFISH WITH PINK PEPPERCORNS

Preserving moist and meaty swordfish with pink peppercorns softens the punchy, sharpness of the lime zest and adds aromatic flavour.

SERVES 6

1 small dried red bird's eye chilli/chile
150 g/5½ oz. sustainably sourced very
   fresh swordfish (or fresh mackerel
   also works)
a few sprigs of fresh coriander/cilantro

PICKLING LIQUOR

80 ml/⅓ cup white wine vinegar
30 g/2½ tablespoons white sugar
1 tablespoon pink peppercorns
finely grated zest of 1 lime
½ tablespoon coriander seeds
a pinch of salt

Mix all the pickling ingredients together in a saucepan with 40 ml/2½ tablespoons water. Set over the heat and bring to the boil. Once boiling, remove from the heat, drop in the dried chilli/chile, pour the mixture into a shallow, non-reactive dish and leave to cool to room temperature. (If you'd like it extra hot, put the chilli/chile in the liquid before boiling.)

   Skin the swordfish, then slice the flesh at an angle to create slices each about 5 mm/¼ inch thick. Place these into the cooled pickling liquid. Sprinkle over the fresh coriander/cilantro and chill for 1 hour before serving.

BARBECUE

PICO DE GALLO

Mexican in origin and made with only a handful of ingredients, this salsa is fresh, vibrant, sharp, fiery and salty all at once – just exactly what you need at a barbecue. The secret to its success is restraint. I deviate slightly from tradition by adding fresh mint and lime zest as well as juice, but apart from that I've kept it classic because it works.

MAKES 1 BOWL TO SHARE

1 white or red onion, finely diced
finely grated zest of 1 lime
4 tablespoons freshly squeezed lime juice
3 ripe medium tomatoes

leaves from a small bunch of fresh coriander/cilantro, chopped
leaves from a small bunch of fresh mint, chopped
1 fresh green jalapeño chilli/chile, deseeded and finely diced
¼ teaspoon salt, or more to taste

Put the onion, lime zest and lime juice in a mixing bowl, mix together and leave to steep.

Quarter and deseed the tomatoes and dice the flesh. Tip the cubed flesh into a sieve/strainer set over a bowl to allow the juices to drain off.

Add the drained diced tomatoes, coriander/cilantro, mint, jalapeño and the salt to the onion and lime juice mixture in the bowl. Stir together and taste just before serving in case it needs more salt or lime juice. This, and My Mum's Avocado Salsa (opposite) work with just about everything that comes off a grill.

MY MUM'S AVOCADO SALSA

I stole this recipe from my Mum and make no apologies for it – she's
an amazing cook and we always have this at our barbecues. It's chunky,
rustic and packs a huge flavour punch. Don't be shy with the olive oil...

MAKES 1 BOWL TO SHARE

60 ml/¼ cup extra-virgin olive oil
2 tablespoons distilled malt vinegar
1 garlic clove, crushed
a pinch of dried oregano
1 ripe avocado, pitted and coarsely diced

2 ripe tomatoes, diced
a handful of freshly chopped coriander/
  cilantro
2 spring onions/scallions, finely sliced
1 fresh red jalapeño chilli/chile, deseeded
  and finely diced
salt and freshly ground black pepper

Put the olive oil, vinegar, garlic and oregano in a small bowl and whisk until
emulsified (or pop it all in a jar with a lid and shake vigorously, much easier...).

Put the rest of the ingredients in a mixing bowl, fold together, then pour over
the dressing. Taste to see if it needs more vinegar or oil before serving.

EMBER-ROASTED CORN WITH CAYENNE BUTTER

Cooking cobs of corn in their husks directly on the coals gives them a wonderful smokiness and, let's face it, it's a pretty cool way to serve them too. Add a smear of my salty cayenne butter for a little spicy kick. This method is also great for campfire cooking... just throw the cobs in when the flames have died down.

MAKES 6

6 cobs of fresh sweetcorn (husks on)
150 g/1¼ sticks butter, softened
1 tablespoon sea salt flakes, or to taste
1 teaspoon cayenne pepper, or to taste

Preheat the barbecue/outdoor grill to hot/high.

Meanwhile, soak the cobs in water for 30 minutes, this will stop the husks burning too quickly and the residual moisture will help steam the kernels. While you are waiting, you can make the cayenne butter.

Put the softened butter in a mixing bowl with the salt flakes and cayenne pepper and beat until blended. Taste, adding more salt or cayenne to suit your own taste. Scrape the butter into a small bowl and level the surface with the back of a spoon. Chill in the fridge until ready to use.

When you are ready to cook the corn, shake the excess water from the cobs and place them directly onto the coals, you want just the burning embers, no flames. They take about 30 minutes to cook; turn them every so often when the husks have fully blackened, then remove from the heat and rest for a few minutes. If you're using a gas barbecue/outdoor grill, place above the hottest part of the barbecue/grill.

To remove the husks in one go, use a sharp knife and cut the base off the corn, leave a couple of corn on the cob with the husks on and just pulled back to reveal the corn, basically because this looks cool! You can tie them back with string to keep things nice and tidy, if you like.

Serve in a pile on the sharing board, letting a few tablespoons of the salty cayenne butter melt over the top of the hot corn and the rest spread next to the corn – directly onto the board is how I like to do it.

CHARRED CAESAR SALAD

I was introduced to the concept of barbecuing salad when my wife and I were visiting some friends on Vancouver Island. It totally changes the texture and delivers a delicate smokiness that I just love and the leaves stand up to the heat with the bravery of a firefighter! The secret here is to grill the leaves until they are well charred and the cheese is crispy.

SERVES 4

60 ml/¼ cup olive oil, plus extra for frying breadcrumbs
1 thick slice of seeded bread
2 Romaine/Cos lettuces
salt and freshly ground black pepper

CAESAR DRESSING

1 garlic clove, crushed
60 ml/¼ cup good-quality mayonnaise
½ tablespoon freshly squeezed lemon juice
30 g/scant ½ cup finely grated Parmesan
½ teaspoon clear, runny honey
3 canned anchovy fillets, finely chopped

Preheat the barbecue/outdoor grill to hot/high.

To make nice, rustic croutons, drizzle a little olive oil over the slice of bread, season it with salt and pepper and toast on the barbecue/grill, to the side of the coals, for a few minutes on each side until it has a deep golden hue then remove it and set aside to cool down.

Put all the caesar dressing ingredients in a bowl and whisk together to combine. Set aside until needed.

Halve the lettuces lengthways and spoon a couple of tablespoons of the caesar dressing over the cut side. Lift a few leaves and prize them open a little to get some of the dressing deeper inside, but don't smother them.

Place the lettuce halves, dressing side-down, onto the hot barbecue/grill over direct heat and cook for about 4 minutes, or until the leaves are charred. You'll lose some of the dressing onto the barbecue/grill and it will start to smoke – that's all good. Turn the lettuces over and cook for a few minutes more on the other side, then remove from the heat. Place the lettuce leaves onto your board. Rip the toast into small chunks and scatter these over the top.

GREEK-STYLE LAMB CHOPS

This tasty recipe will add a uniquely Greek touch to your barbecue.
It's traditionally served well done – the crispy fat is the best bit!

SERVES 4

1 kg/2 lb. 4 oz. lamb chops
freshly chopped flat-leaf parsley, to serve
salt flakes, to sprinkle
1 lemon, cut into wedges, for squeezing

LEMON, GARLIC AND HERB MARINADE
a small bunch of fresh thyme
finely grated zest and freshly squeezed
   juice of 1 lemon
2 tablespoons dried oregano
2 garlic cloves, crushed
125 ml/½ cup olive oil (ideally Greek!)
1 teaspoon each salt and black pepper

Preheat the barbecue/outdoor grill to hot/high.

Meanwhile, put the lamb chops in a shallow dish. Reserve a few sprigs of
thyme to garnish and strip the leaves off the rest. Put the leaves in a small bowl
with the rest of the marinade ingredients and mix. Pour over the lamb, cover and
marinate in the fridge for 2 hours (removing the dish 30 minutes before cooking).

Shake the excess marinade off the lamb and reserve it. Put the chops straight
onto the hot barbecue/grill and cook for 5–7 minutes on each side (depending
on their thickness), basting in the reserved marinade throughout cooking.

Serve in a stack with the reserved thyme, the parsley, salt and lemon wedges.

LEMONGRASS-MARINATED STEAKS

I spent some time travelling in South-east Asia and fell in love with the flavours you encounter there. This lovely marinade, heavy on the fish sauce, lemongrass and chilli/chile really complements red meat. I like to keep some back to use as a dressing and drizzle it over the cooked steak, throwing the flavour barometer into overdrive! Worth noting that this goes particularly well with a cold bottle of beer – but then doesn't everything at a barbecue/cook out?

SERVES 4

4 x 200-g/7-oz. dry-aged rump steaks

LEMONGRASS MARINADE
4 lemongrass sticks
4 tablespoons fish sauce
finely grated zest of ½ lime
3 tablespoons freshly squeezed lime juice
1 tablespoon soft brown sugar
1 fresh red bird's eye chilli/chile, sliced
2 tablespoons olive oil
a pinch of salt

Preheat the barbecue/outdoor grill to hot/high.

To make the marinade, trim the lemongrass sticks, crush each one with the flat side of a knife and finely chop. Put in a jug/pitcher with the rest of the marinade ingredients and add the salt. Mix to combine.

Lay the steaks on a flat plate or tray and smother with half of the marinade. Reserve the remaining marinade – you'll be using this as a dressing later for the cooked meat. Cover the steaks loosely and marinate in the fridge for 1 hour, or overnight if you are sufficiently organized! Take them out of the fridge 30 minutes before you want to cook them, to bring them back to room temperature.

When ready to cook, put the steaks directy onto the hot barbecue/grill and give them about 4–5 minutes on each side for medium (but you can, of course, cook them for slightly less or more time to suit your own preference).

Remove the steaks from the heat, let them rest for 5 minutes, then carve each one widthways into three pieces. Pour or spoon over the reserved marinade, then open that cold beer and enjoy.

BLACKENED MACKEREL FILLETS WITH GREMOLATA

Mackerel is a delight to cook on the barbecue/grill. It does need to be fresh (it doesn't freeze well) and cooked over a harsh, dry heat to help crisp and slightly blacken its gleaming silver skin. Cooked this way, it needs nothing more than the citrusy tang of lemon zest combined with some chopped flat-leaf parsley and garlic to balance the oiliness of the fish. A simple Mediterranean classic, perfect for a sunny day.

SERVES 6 TO SHARE, 3 AS A MAIN

6 fresh mackerel fillets, skin-on
sea salt flakes

GREMOLATA
4 tablespoons finely chopped flat-leaf
   parsley leaves

finely grated zest and freshly squeezed
   juice of 1 lemon
2 garlic cloves, finely chopped
olive oil, for drizzling and grilling

Preheat the barbecue/outdoor grill to hot/high.

To make the gremolata, mix together the parsley, lemon zest and garlic in a small bowl. Stir in the lemon juice and a tiny drizzle of olive oil (it's not meant to be runny, add just enough oil to coat the other ingredients), and set aside until needed.

Lightly oil the barbecue/outdoor grill rack, salt the mackerel skin and place the fillets, skin-side down, over direct heat.

Leave the fillets to cook for about 6–8 minutes, until the skin is crispy and almost blackened – this will cook the mackerel flesh almost all the way through. Turn the fillets over and cook for just 30 seconds or so to finish the other side off then remove from the barbecue/grill.

Arrange the blackened mackerel fillets on your board or serving platter, skin-side up, squeeze over the remaining lemon juice and spoon over about half of the gremolata. Serve the rest straight on your board or in a small bowl on the side for guests to help themselves.

CHICKEN SOUVLAKI WITH DATE MOLASSES & TAHINI DRESSING

I prefer to use chicken thigh meat for my souvlaki for maximum flavour and also because it can be cooked until the pieces are crisp on the outside whilst still remaining succulent. Date molasses is a rich, silky syrup extracted from dates that has a sweet caramel flavour. Once combined with hot mustard and garlic, it makes a balanced sauce to slather over your chicken before it hits the barbecue/grill. Serve these skewers with a versatile tahini dressing that has the magic combination of sharp creamy yogurt with the nutty earthiness of sesame seeds. It works particularly well with any grilled dish and gets along very nicely with other popular Middle Eastern flavours like sumac, fresh coriander/cilantro and pomegranate seeds.

MAKES 4 SKEWERS

CHICKEN SOUVLAKI
90 ml/⅓ cup date molasses
30 ml/2 tablespoons English/hot
    mustard
½ garlic clove, crushed
1 tablespoon olive oil, plus extra
    to drizzle
600 g/1 lb. 5 oz. boneless, skinless
    chicken thighs, cut into bite-sized
    chunks (you need about 30 pieces)
1 courgette/zucchini, halved lengthways,
    then sliced into 2-cm/¾-inch pieces

salt and freshly ground black pepper
a handful of freshly chopped coriander/
    cilantro leaves, to garnish

TAHINI DRESSING
½ tablespoon tahini paste
4 tablespoons thick Greek yogurt
1 tablespoon freshly squeezed lemon
    juice
salt and ground white pepper, to season
sumac, to dust (optional)

4 large wooden skewers, pre-soaked
    in water

Preheat the barbecue/outdoor grill to hot/high.

To make the glaze, put the date molasses, mustard, garlic, olive oil and a pinch of salt in a mixing bowl and mix thoroughly to combine. Decant one-third of the mixture into a separate small bowl and reserve to use later.

Add the chicken pieces to the mixing bowl and toss them in the glaze. You can leave the chicken to marinate overnight in the fridge, but I'm never that prepared, so mix and cook is my motto!

To assemble the souvlaki, thread a couple pieces of chicken, then a chunk of courgette/zucchini onto each skewer and keep going until all is used and you have four skewers ready to cook. Season with a few turns of black pepper, add a tiny drizzle of olive oil and place the skewers on the hot barbecue/outdoor grill (or under a hot grill/broiler, if preferred, but you must have the grill/broiler preheated to as hot as possible.)

Cook the skewers for about 8 minutes, or until they start to char, before turning over, and continue until they have been cooking for about 15 minutes in total. About 5 minutes before they finish cooking, brush over some of the decanted glaze that hasn't touched the raw chicken to give them an extra kick of flavour. You can test to see if the chicken is cooked by cutting a piece open. It should be white and hot throughout.

Stack the skewers on your sharing board, drizzle over any remaining glaze and scatter the fresh coriander/cilantro over the top to garnish.

To make the tahini dressing, simply mix the tahini, yogurt and lemon juice together in a bowl with a little salt and pepper. Taste and add more of any of the ingredients until you get your preferred flavour. Add a splash of water if you want a looser dressing. Transfer to a serving dish and dust the surface lightly with sumac (if using), or simply drizzle the dresing over the skewers once they are arranged on the serving board.

SPICY PORK BURGERS WITH CUCUMBER RELISH

I'm a big fan of burgers cooked on the barbecue, but sometimes I want something with a little more kick and fresher tasting and that's exactly when I make these. Packed with summery vibes and a few South-east Asian aromatics, they are a departure from the norm and a real treat.

MAKES 2 LARGE BURGERS

250 g/9 oz. minced/ground pork
7.5-cm/3-inch piece of root ginger, grated
2 garlic cloves, grated
2 lemongrass sticks, finely chopped
2 fresh green bird's eye chillies/chiles, finely sliced
freshly squeezed juice and finely grated zest of 2 limes
4 tablespoons fish sauce
4 spring onions/scallions, finely sliced
a handful of freshly chopped mint leaves
a handful of freshly chopped coriander/ cilantro leaves
1 tablespoon olive oil, plus extra for oiling the burgers
2 tablespoons grated cucumber, juice squeezed out as much as possible
a pinch of soft brown sugar
2 tablespoons sweet chilli/chili sauce
1 large brioche burger bun, halved and lightly toasted on the cut side only
salt and freshly ground black pepper

Preheat the barbecue/outdoor grill to hot/high.

Put the minced/ground pork in a mixing bowl and add the ginger, garlic, lemongrass, one chilli/chile, half the lime zest and juice, half the fish sauce, half the spring onions/scallions and half the freshly chopped mint and coriander/ cilantro. Season with a little salt and pepper, and fold together until well combined, but try not to overwork the meat.

Use your hands to form the mixture into two large patties and lightly oil the outside of each one.

Place the burgers on the hot barbecue/grill and cook for about 6–8 minutes on each side, or until the juices run clear. For some reason, people seem to have a habit of pushing down on burgers with a spatula whilst they're cooking; all this does is squeeze the juices out and results in a dry burger. Stop it! Leave the patties well alone until they are ready to be turned over.

To make the fresh cucumber relish, put the grated cucumber in a bowl. Add the remaining chilli/chile, lime zest and juice, fish sauce, spring onions/scallions and herbs, and the sugar and olive oil. Spoon a little sweet chilli/chili sauce onto each bun half, followed by a hot burger and a spoonful of the cucumber relish.

MAPLE & MUSTARD-GLAZED RAINBOW CARROTS

These colourful carrots in shades of autumn/fall leaves are only briefly cooked on a high heat so that they retain a little pleasing bite. The warming sticky maple and spicy mustard glaze makes them perfect for your harvest board.

SERVES 6

500 g/1 lb. 2 oz. long, thin rainbow carrots, each about 2.5 cm/1 inch diameter
2 tablespoons pure maple syrup
1 tablespoon wholegrain mustard
½ teaspoon English/hot mustard
½ teaspoon clear, runny honey
1 teaspoon apple cider vinegar
salt and freshly ground black pepper
fresh flat-leaf parsley sprigs, to garnish

Preheat the oven to 200°C (400°F) Gas 6.
  Wash the carrots and cut them in half lengthways, leaving some of the green stalk intact if you can.
  Put all the remaining ingredients, except the parsley, salt and pepper, in a large mixing bowl and whisk until combined. Add the carrots to the bowl and toss them to coat in the glaze.
  Put the glazed carrots on a baking sheet, pour over any remaining glaze, season with a pinch each of salt and pepper and roast in the preheated oven for about 20 minutes. Serve on your board, garnished with parsley sprigs.

ROSEMARY & RED ONION ROASTED BABY NEW POTATOES

The warming and woody aromas of rosemary, caramelized red onion and garlic keep these little roasties company in this one-pan recipe. Once cooked, pile them high on your harvest board; the addition of a few extra sprigs of fresh rosemary to garnish is a nice touch.

SERVES 8

about 1 kg/2 lb. 4 oz. new potatoes, unpeeled and scrubbed
6 small red onions, peeled and each cut into 4 or 6 wedges
2 whole garlic bulbs, left unpeeled and halved horizontally

4 tablespoons olive oil
needles stripped from 12 sprigs of fresh rosemary, plus extra sprigs to garnish
salt and freshly ground black pepper
sea salt flakes, to sprinkle

a deep-sided roasting pan or sheet pan

Preheat the oven to 180°C (350°F) Gas 4 .

Cut any larger new potatoes in half so they are all of a similar size and drop them into your roasting pan or sheet pan. Add the red onions and halved garlic bulbs. Coat everything with the olive oil, shake the pan and season generously with salt and pepper. Rub the rosemary leaves between the palms of your hands to release the oils and drop half of them into the pan to join the rest of the ingredients.

Roast in the preheated oven for about 45 minutes, or until the potatoes are cooked through and golden; give the tray a shake halfway through cooking to stop them from sticking to the base.

Remove from the oven, scatter over the remaining rosemary needles and sprinkle over some salt flakes. Arrange on your board in piles and garnish with extra rosemary sprigs before serving.

ROAST SQUASH & LENTIL SALAD

This is simple to make and such a satisfying dish to eat on colder days. Serve it as part of your harvest board or enjoy it on its own as a warming supper. The sweet butternut squash contrasts nicely with the dark and earthy lentils, both in flavour and appearance. If you've got some feta lurking in the fridge, throw a few crumbs on top to serve.

SERVES 8 TO SHARE, 4 AS A MAIN

1 x 1-kg/2-lb. 4 oz. winter squash, such as butternut, pumpkin, hubbard or acorn
about 4 tablespoons olive oil
a couple of pinches of dried oregano
a few sprigs of fresh rosemary
6 garlic cloves, unpeeled and halved
1 x 250-g/9-oz. packet of ready-to-eat cooked Puy lentils
1 x 250-g/9-oz. packet of ready-to-eat cooked green lentils
½ red onion, thinly sliced
100 g/3½ oz. cooked beetroot/beet, cut into wedges
a small handful freshly chopped flat-leaf parsley
about 2 tablespoons red wine vinegar, to taste
salt and freshly ground black pepper

Preheat the oven to 200°C (400°F) Gas 6.

Peel and deseed the squash and cut the flesh into 2.5-cm/1-inch slices (if you are using butternut, you can leave the skin on as it will cook okay). Put the squash pieces in a bowl and add a glug of olive oil, the oregano, rosemary and garlic.

Tip into a roasting pan and roast in the preheated oven for about 30 minutes, or until the squash is tender and cooked and starting to brown at the edges.

Tip both the Puy and green lentils into a large bowl and add the red onion, beetroot/beet wedges and chopped parsley. Dress the salad with a generous amount of the remaining olive oil and a splash of red wine vinegar – taste and adjust the balance of olive oil and vinegar to taste. Season with salt and pepper.

Add the roasted squash to the bowl and fold it into the lentils, along with any cooking juices in the pan. Serve straight onto your board or in a serving bowl.

GRIDDLED PEAR & BLUE CHEESE SALAD

Here's a warm salad of pan-griddled pears lounging on crisp chicory/ Belgian endive and dotted with nuggets of tangy blue cheese and toasted pine nuts, it's delicious in its own right and also perfectly complements the array of rich foods on this comforting board.

SERVES 8 TO SHARE

4 Green Williams/Bartlett pears, washed and patted dry
250 g/9 oz. chicory/Belgian endive
45 ml/3 tablespoons olive oil

30 ml/2 tablespoons sherry vinegar
45 g/⅓ cup pine nut kernels
200 g/7 oz. any smooth, tangy soft blue cheese (I use Blacksticks Blue)
salt and freshly ground black pepper

Preheat a heavy metal ridged griddle/grill pan until hot.

Halve the pears and cut each half into four to give you eight thin wedges. Cut out the tough cores. Lay the pear wedges directly into the pan and leave them to sizzle for about 4–5 minutes, until charred, then turn over and cook the other side for a further 4–5 minutes on the other side. Once done, transfer them to a large mixing bowl.

Separate the chicory/Belgian endive leaves and add them to the bowl with the warm pears. Drizzle over the olive oil and vinegar and gently fold together, taking care not to break up the pears. Set aside.

Dry toast the pine nut kernels in a small frying pan/skillet for a few minutes until browned, then add these to the bowl with the pears.

Season the salad with salt and pepper and use your fingertips to crumble in pieces of the blue cheese. Transfer the salad straight onto your board or into a large flat serving dish, letting any excess liquid drain off as you lift it. Serve whilst still warm.

CHEESE FONDUE WITH SALMON & PROSECCO

Harvest-time isn't all about heavy, robust stews. Served in a whole roasted pumpkin, this luxurious salmon fondue is laced with sparkling Prosecco which creates air in the mixture and delivers a deliciously light texture. Serve with cubes of bread to swirl around in the sauce.

SERVES 6

a 2-kg/4-lb. 8-oz. pumpkin (optional)
60 ml/¼ cup olive oil
35 g/¼ cup plain/all-purpose flour
450 ml/2 scant cups full-fat/whole milk
1 dried or fresh bay leaf
a generous pinch of ground nutmeg
a pinch of mild curry powder

150 g/1⅔ cups grated mature/sharp
  Cheddar or Parmesan
500 g/1 lb. 2 oz. skinless, boneless salmon
  fillets, cut into bite-sized cubes
30 ml/2 tablespoons Prosecco
leaves from a small bunch of flat-leaf
  parsley, freshly chopped
salt and freshly ground black pepper
cubed bread, to serve

Preheat the oven to 200°C (400°F) Gas 6.

Start by roasting your serving pumpkin (if using). Slice the top off the pumpkin about 5 cm/2 inches from the top, saving the 'lid'. Scrape out the seeds from inside with a spoon and discard them. Season inside the pumpkin with salt and pepper, place both the pumpkin and the top on a baking sheet and roast in the preheated oven for 25 minutes, then remove and set aside. Turn the oven off.

To make the fondue, put the oil and flour into a saucepan, combine and bring to a simmer to cook out the flour for a few minutes, then remove from the heat. Pour in the milk, stir thoroughly, add the bay leaf, nutmeg and curry powder and season with salt and pepper. Bring back to a simmer, stirring continuously. Once the mixture starts to bubble, stir in the grated cheese and then introduce the salmon cubes, gently folding them in rather than stirring and being careful not to break them up. Cook for 2 minutes, then remove from the heat. Pour in the Prosecco and the chopped parsley and again, gently fold in.

Place the cooked pumpkin (if using) in position on your board and carefully pour in the hot fondue mixture and pop the 'hat' back on the pumpkin at a jaunty angle (or pour the fondue into a serving bowl). Serve with a pile of cubed bread on the side ready for dunking.

SKILLET CORNBREAD WITH PADRÓN PEPPERS

Cornbread is so easy to make and can be put together in 30 minutes from start to finish, and flavoured with whatever you like. Recipes vary across America; they say in the North they make it crumblier and less sweet, and in the Southern states it's a little softer and sweeter. I have to admit, I prefer it the Southern way! And when I bake it myself, I add a good hit of cheese and stud it with padrón peppers – it works a treat and makes it the ideal sharer for this board. That said, I strongly recommend eating it still warm from the pan with lashings of butter...

SERVES 8

150 g/1 cup cornmeal/polenta
120 g/1 cup plain/all-purpose flour
½ teaspoon salt
1 teaspoon sugar
1 tablespoon baking powder
90 g/1 cup grated mature/sharp Cheddar
1 tablespoon fresh thyme leaves
1 egg
250 ml/1 cup full-fat/whole milk

1 tablespoon apple cider vinegar
80 ml/⅓ cup olive oil, plus extra
   for drizzling
a knob/pat of butter
about 6 Padrón (or piquillo) peppers,
   sliced lengthways and deseeded
sea salt flakes, to sprinkle

*a 25-cm/10-inch cast-iron ovenproof
   skillet (or alternatively, you can use
   a metal roasting pan)*

Preheat the oven to 200°C (400°F) Gas 6 and place the skillet in the oven to heat.

Put the cornmeal/polenta, flour, salt, sugar, baking powder, grated cheese and two-thirds of the thyme leaves in a mixing bowl and stir to combine.

In a separate bowl, combine the egg, milk, vinegar and oil and whisk together. Pour these wet ingredients into the bowl with the dry ingredients and mix until you have a smooth, thick batter, rather than a dough.

Take the skillet out of the oven (use an oven glove and be very careful – it's hot!). Drop the butter into the pan and swirl it around until melted and then pour in the batter. Scatter the remaining thyme leaves and the peppers over the top and sprinkle with sea salt flakes. Give it a drizzle of olive oil and pop it into the preheated oven for 20 minutes, or until a knife comes out clean. Leave to cool and then enjoy. And don't forget to have the butter within easy reach if you want to sneak a piece before anyone else gets to it!

PORK & MULLED CIDER CASSEROLE

It simply doesn't come any more autumnal than this casserole! Pork shoulder slow-cooked in an aromatic, deliciously tangy yet slightly sweet mulled cider sauce and served inside a whole roasted pumpkin...

SERVES 6

a 2-kg/4-lb. 8 oz. pumpkin (optional)
600 g/1 lb. 5 oz. pork shoulder/Boston butt, cubed
50 g/2 oz. smoked lardons
1 white onion, diced
1 celery stick, diced
2 garlic cloves, sliced
2 tablespoons plain/all-purpose flour
500 ml/2 cups dry (hard) cider
1 tablespoon apple cider vinegar
1 apple, cored and cut into chunks
1 tablespoon Dijon mustard
1 tablespoon pure maple syrup
a few sprigs of fresh thyme
3 fresh or dried bay leaves
6 cloves
2 star anise
1 small cinnamon stick
salt and freshly ground black pepper
olive oil, for frying and drizzling

Preheat the oven to 200°C (400°F) Gas 6.

Start by roasting your serving pumpkin (if using). Slice the top off the pumpkin about 5 cm/2 inches from the top, saving the 'lid'. Scrape out the seeds from inside with a spoon and discard them. Season inside the pumpkin with salt and pepper, place both the pumpkin and the top on a baking sheet and roast in the preheated oven for 25 minutes, then remove and set aside. Reduce the oven to 180°C (350°F) Gas 4, ready for the casserole.

To make the casserole, heat a generous glug of olive oil in a large saucepan. Add the cubed pork shoulder/Boston butt and fry/sauté to gently brown all over. Remove from the pan, transfer to a bowl, cover and set aside until needed.

Add the lardons to the same pan (no need to clean it) and fry/sauté until crispy. Add the onion, celery and garlic and cook for 5 minutes, until the onion is translucent. Stir in the flour, ensuring it is well incorporated into the onion mixture, then pour in the cider. Add the vinegar, apple, mustard, maple syrup, thyme, bay leaves and all the spices, and finally put the browned pork shoulder/ Boston butt back into the pan, pouring in any meat juices from the bowl.

Stir, and cook in the oven for 1½ hours, then rest for 10 minutes before serving. Position the pumpkin (if using) on your board and ladle in the casserole, pop the 'lid' back on the pumpkin, stand back and gaze in awe at your creation.

SMOKY CHICKEN & BLACK BEAN STEW

As soon as the leaves turn colour and there is a chill in the air, I start craving comfort food, and this seductively earthy chicken and black bean stew always hits the spot for me, so I'm happy to share it with you.

SERVES 6

a 2-kg/4-lb. 8-oz. pumpkin (optional)
900 g/2 lb. chicken thighs, skinned and deboned
100 g/3½ oz. cooking chorizo, diced
1 white onion, diced
2 garlic cloves, sliced
1 fresh jalapeño chilli/chile, chopped
1 tablespoon smoked paprika
5 fresh or dried bay leaves
1 tablespoon dried thyme

a generous splash of white wine
100 g/½ cup chopped tomatoes
2 tablespoons tomato purée/paste
200 g/1 cup dried black turtle beans (no need to soak or pre-cook these)
850 ml/3½ cups good chicken stock
1 tablespoon apple cider vinegar
a pinch of sugar
a small bunch each of flat-leaf parsley and coriander/cilantro, chopped
salt and freshly ground black pepper
olive oil, for frying

Preheat the oven to 200°C (400°F) Gas 6.

Start by roasting your serving pumpkin (if using). Slice the top off the pumpkin about 5 cm/2 inches from the top, saving the 'lid'. Scrape out the seeds from inside with a spoon and discard them. Season inside the pumpkin with salt and pepper, place both the pumpkin and the top on a baking sheet and roast in the preheated oven for 25 minutes, then remove and set aside. Reduce the oven to 160°C (325°F) Gas 3, ready for the stew.

To make the stew, heat a glug of olive oil in a lidded casserole dish. Season the chicken with salt and pepper, add to the dish and fry/sauté until golden all over. Remove from the dish, transfer to a bowl, cover and set aside until needed.

In the same dish, fry the chorizo for a few minutes, until all the red oil is released. Add the onion and cook for a few minutes before adding the garlic and chilli/chile. After 1 minute, add the paprika, bay leaves, thyme and wine. Simmer until the wine has almost all evaporated, then add the chopped tomatoes, tomato purée/paste and black beans. Stir well before adding the stock, vinegar and sugar and season to taste. Return the chicken to the dish, pouring in any juices from the bowl. Cover with the lid, cook in the preheated oven for 2 hours, then rest for 10 minutes before adding the herbs. Serve in the pumpkin (if using).

FEAST

BITE-SIZED VEGETABLE ROLLS WITH HALLOUMI

Strips of charred aubergine/eggplant are wrapped around a host of tastes and textures that will keep you coming back for more. They do tend to bring out a greedy streak in most people so make plenty.

MAKES ABOUT 16

60 g/2 oz. white cabbage, shredded
60 g/2 oz. raw beetroot/beet, peeled and grated
a handful each of fresh coriander/ cilantro and mint leaves, coarsely chopped
1 tablespoon freshly squeezed lemon juice

2 aubergines/eggplants
200 g/7 oz. halloumi
4 tablespoons hummus
4 tablespoons toasted almonds, coarsely crushed
2 tablespoons pomegranate seeds
salt and freshly ground black pepper
olive oil, for drizzling
clear, runny honey, for drizzling
pomegranate molasses, for drizzling

Combine the shredded cabbage, grated beetroot/beet and chopped herbs in a bowl and add a squeeze of lemon juice, a pinch each of salt and pepper and a small drizzle of olive oil.

Slice the aubergines/eggplants lengthways as finely as you can get them (about 3 mm/^{1}/8 inch is ideal) and aim for 16 slices. Heat a non-strick griddle/grill pan until hot and cook the strips for about 2 minutes on each side. Repeat until all 16 are done and set aside.

Keeping the griddle/grill pan hot, cut the halloumi widthways into 15-mm/^{1}/2-inch thick slices and then in half again lengthways to create batons. Place these in the griddle/grill pan and cook for 2 minutes on each side, or until nicely charred. (If you haven't got a non-stick pan, you can brush the halloumi with a little olive oil before cooking it).

To assemble the rolls, lay the aubergine/eggplant slices out flat and spread a teaspoon of hummus over each one. Place a halloumi baton at one end, a heaped tablespoon of the cabbage mixture on top. Add a few drops of honey and a pinch of almonds and pomegranate seeds. Roll the aubergine/eggplant up. Repeat until all 16 are done. Arrange them on a platter, seam-side down, and drizzle with pomegranate molasses and more honey, if liked. Scatter any pomegranate seeds, almonds and herbs still lurking on your chopping board over the top and serve.

HOME-BAKED SODA BREAD

Homemade bread is a humble treat that I'm always grateful for. That said, I rarely have the time (or patience) to prove dough, which is why I like this recipe that can be baked straight away. Keep it simple to serve with dukkah, but add rosemary and garlic to the dough another time.

MAKES 1 LOAF (8 SERVINGS)

500 g/4 cups plain/all-purpose flour, plus extra for dusting
½ tablespoon bicarbonate of soda/baking soda
1 teaspoon salt

215 g/1 cup thick Greek yogurt
250 ml/1 cup full-fat/whole milk
2 tablespoons clear, runny honey
60 ml/¼ cup extra-virgin olive oil
needles from a sprig of fresh rosemary (optional)
2 crushed garlic cloves (optional)

Preheat the oven to 200°C (400°F) Gas 6. Dust a baking sheet with flour.

Put the flour, bicarbonate of soda/baking soda and salt in a large mixing bowl and stir to combine.

Whisk together the yogurt, milk, honey and oil and then slowly fold this into the dry ingredients in the mixing bowl, until you have a slightly sticky dough. (Add the rosemary needles and crushed garlic at this stage, if using.)

Turn the dough out onto a lightly flour-dusted surface and knead it just enough to bring it together into a round. Pop it onto the prepared baking sheet, flattening it slightly, use a sharp knife to score across the top four times, as if they are spokes in a wheel. Bake in the preheated oven for about 30 minutes, or until the loaf sounds hollow when you tap it on the base. Serve warm.

BITTER CHOCOLATE DUKKAH

What could feel more decadent than an ancient Egyptian condiment of toasted nuts and spices gracing your feast board? Dukkah recipes vary from home to home, but I like the richness of dark chocolate with the aromatic toasted spices and heat from Aleppo flakes. To eat, dunk a piece of soda bread into golden oil then into the dukkah. Heady stuff.

MAKES ABOUT 130 G/1 CUP

2 tablespoons whole almonds
1 tablespoon pine nut kernels
1 tablespoon sesame seeds
½ tablespoon cumin seeds
½ teaspoon fennel seeds
½ tablespoon coriander seeds

a pinch of smoked paprika
½ tablespoon grated dark/bittersweet
  chocolate (80% cocoa solids)
a generous pinch of Aleppo pepper flakes
a small pinch of caster/superfine sugar
a generous pinch of sea salt flakes
Home-baked Soda Bread (see opposite)
  and good olive oil, to serve

Dry toast the almonds and pine nuts in a frying pan/skillet for a few minutes just until they start to colour, then add the sesame seeds for the last minute. Tip into a bowl and leave to cool.

In the same dry pan, toast the cumin, fennel and coriander seeds for a couple of minutes, until they release their aroma, then remove them from the heat and add to the nuts in the bowl.

Once all the nuts and spices are cool, add the smoked paprika then transfer the mixture to a food processor and pulse until a coarse consistency is achieved. Tip the dukkah back into the bowl and fold in the dark/bittersweet chocolate, Aleppo pepper flakes, sugar and sea salt. Spoon into a screwtop jar and store in the fridge until ready to use. (You can make this without the chocolate to extend its shelf life – just add the chocolate when you are about to serve a portion.)

ULTIMATE ROASTED VEGETABLES

This recipe brings back a lot of childhood memories for me. The magic is in the simple addition of a can of chopped tomatoes, which once cooked, adds sweetness and depth. You can use whatever selection of vegetables you want, but the marrow and red onions are mandatory!

SERVES 6

400 g/14 oz. new potatoes, sliced
 1 cm/³/8 inch thick
1 red onion, sliced but not too finely
200 g/7 oz. cauliflower, broken into
 florets
½ marrow, halved deseded and sliced
 2.5 cm/1 inch thick
1 large carrot, peeled and thinly sliced
1 raw beetroot/beet, peeled and cut
 into chunks

½ red (bell) pepper, deseeded and
 sliced into chunks
½ green (bell) pepper, deseeded and
 sliced into chunks
60 ml/¼ cup olive oil
2 tablespoons dried oregano
200 g/1 cup good-quality chopped
 canned tomatoes
salt and freshly ground black pepper

Preheat the oven to 180°C (350°F) Gas 4.

Place all the prepared vegetables in a large roasting pan or deep-sided sheet pan, big enough to avoid having to pile all the ingredients on top of each other.

Pour over the olive oil, add the oregano and season generously with salt and freshly ground black pepper. Toss all the vegetables with your hands to coat them in the oil and seasoning.

Pour over the canned tomatoes, but don't stir, leave it as it is.

Roast in the preheated oven for 1 hour, then rest for 10 minutes before serving.

TOMATO & BLUE CHEESE SALAD WITH TORN CIABATTA CROUTONS

This is one of my go-to salads – usually because my wife tells me to make it... but also because it's quick to put together and needs just a handful of simple ingredients. But don't let the simplicity fool you; you've got to use the best tomatoes you can buy and a really good cheese; a Shropshire Blue works perfectly, it's tangy like a stilton but slightly creamer with an orange hue. Paradoxically, the ciabatta is best if it's a day or two old, but don't worry if you buy it on the day.

SERVES 6

200 g/7 oz. stale ciabatta bread
a few glugs of olive oil
a pinch of dried chilli/hot red pepper
  flakes
a pinch of dried oregano
100 g/4 oz. wild rocket/arugula
500 g/18 oz. any variety of ripe tomatoes
150 g/6 oz. Shropshire blue cheese
2 tablespoons sherry vinegar
salt and freshly ground black pepper

Preheat the oven to 200°C (400°F) Gas 6.

Tear the ciabatta into chunks and put it in a bowl. Sprinkle over a little olive oil (2–3 tablespoons should do it) and add the chilli/hot red pepper flakes, oregano and salt and pepper. Tip onto a baking sheet and bake in the preheated oven for 5 minutes, or just long enough for the bread to dry out.

Spread the rocket/arugula out evenly over a large platter. Slice or halve the tomatoes, depending on their size, and arrange over the top.

Break up the cheese into marble-sized pieces and scatter these over the tomatoes, no need to toss them in, you want to keep the salad in layers. Season generously with coarsely ground black pepper and a pinch of salt. Dress liberally with olive oil and follow with the vinegar.

Finally, scatter the baked ciabatta croutons over the salad to add a lovely crunch and some extra flavour.

SLOW-COOKED PORK BELLY WITH ROASTED APPLE KETCHUP

I do love a bit of pork belly – it's one of my favourite roasts and it is always greeted with a cheer when I serve it in one whole piece on a board. It's the contrast between the incredibly moist meat and the crisp shards of crackling that does it for me... and here, the pork is roasted on a bed of apples that are smashed into a rich apple ketchup.

SERVES 6

a 2-kg/4-lb. 8-oz. piece of pork belly, skin scored, ideally by your butcher
2 tablespoons vegetable oil
1 white onion, sliced
a few sprigs of fresh rosemary
a few sprigs of fresh thyme
3 fresh or dried bay leaves
6 cloves

3 garlic cloves, whole and lightly cracked
6 apples, halved
250 ml/1 cup white wine
2 tablespoons demerara sugar
1 teaspoon apple cider vinegar
salt and freshly ground black pepper

a large, deep roasting pan, with a good-sized lip

Preheat the oven to 160°C (325°F) Gas 3.

Ask your butcher to score the skin of the pork belly, being careful not to cut through to the meat. Or, if you feel confident, use a sharp knife and do the same yourself – it doesn't need to be pretty, just have lots of cuts to help the skin crisp up. If you can, leave the pork uncovered in a roasting pan in your fridge overnight as this really helps dry out the skin, but don't worry if it's not possible.

Take the meat out of the fridge at least 1 hour before you want to cook it to bring it up to room temperature. Drizzle the vegetable oil over the scored skin of the pork belly, then season it generously with salt and pepper.

Scatter the sliced onions, herb sprigs, bay leaves, cloves and garlic across the bottom of the pan. Arrange the apple halves, cut-side down, and grouped together in the middle of the pan and, pour in the wine and sugar.

Add 125 ml/$\frac{1}{2}$ cup cold water to the pan. Season well with salt and pepper.

Place the pork belly on top of the apples, and roast it in the preheated oven for 3 hours. After that time, whack the temperature up to 200°C (400°F) Gas 6 for about 15 minutes, or until the skin has bubbled and you have a golden roof of crackling over the pork.

Take the pan out of the oven and transfer the pork to a warmed plate and leave it to rest for 15–20 minutes. While the meat is resting, use a potato masher to press all the apples and other ingredients together in the base of the roasting pan – don't worry if there are some burnt bits as it'll only add to the flavour. You can save a few apple halves for garnish before mashing, if liked.

Transfer the mashed apple mixture to a sieve/strainer set over a large bowl. Use the back of a spoon to push it through and you will have a lovely rich apple ketchup in the bowl. Taste it and add more seasoning, sugar or the vinegar, as you feel is necessary.

Place the pork belly on a serving board and smear some apple ketchup alongside it. Spoon the rest into a serving bowl and set alongside for people to help themselves. A good, sharp carving knife and fork need to be close by, ready to serve.

COFFEE-GLAZED SIDE OF SALMON

I remember my auntie doing a side of salmon at Christmas and always thinking 'wow – that's so decadent!'. My moist, coffee-glazed salmon side is perfect as part of your feast board; the subtle, toasted bitterness of the coffee balanced with the sweetness of the sticky honey really works, as unlikely as it sounds, and I tested the recipe plenty of times just to make sure! Serve with charred lemons.

SERVES 8 AS A SHARER, 4 AS A MAIN

125 ml/½ cup freshly brewed espresso coffee
2½ tablespoons clear, runny honey
a pinch of salt
1 tablespoon tomato purée/paste

a 750-g/1-lb. 10-oz. side of boned salmon, skin on
3 lemons, halved
1 tablespoon icing/confectioners' sugar

a large baking sheet, lightly oiled

Preheat the oven to 200°C (400°F) Gas 6.

Put the coffee, honey, salt and tomato purée/paste in a small saucepan and bring to a boil over high heat, then simmer until reduced by about a third, or just until it starts to thicken.

Remove the pan from the heat and let the glaze cool – it will thicken a little more as it does. Place the side of salmon on the lightly oiled baking sheet and liberally spoon over the coffee glaze to cover it. Roast the salmon in the preheated oven for 20–25 minutes, until cooked but still tender and moist.

While the salmon is cooking, heat a frying pan/skillet until hot. Dip the lemon halves in a little icing/confectioners' sugar and put them in the pan, cut-side down. Cook them for a just a few minutes until lightly charred and the sugar has burnt. Set aside.

Remove the salmon from the oven, spoon any leftover coffee glaze from the baking sheet over it. Serve whole on a board, with the charred lemons arranged around it, for squeezing. Encourage everyone to carve and help themselves.

SWEET

POACHED PLUM & CARDAMOM PAVLOVA

I love a good pavlova – here is a cloud of crisp, soft-centred meringue cradling luxurious whipped cream and crowned with sour-sweet poached plums. This is meant to crack, I want the fruit juice to drizzle over the broken edges of the meringue and meander over the board.

SERVES 8 (OR 6 IF GREEDY)

4 egg whites
200 g/1 cup caster/superfine sugar
1 teaspoon freshly squeezed lemon juice
1 teaspoon cornflour/cornstarch
½ tablespoon ground cardamom
400 ml/scant 1¾ cups double/heavy
   cream
a few drops of pure vanilla extract

POACHED PLUMS
6 plums, halved and pitted
100 g/½ cup caster/granulated sugar
250 ml/1 cup white wine
1 cinnamon stick

an electric hand whisk
a baking sheet lined with baking
   parchment (use a pencil to draw a
   template around a dinner plate on it)

Preheat the oven to 140°C (275°F) Gas 1.

To make the poached plums, put the plums, sugar, wine and cinnamon stick in a large saucepan and set over a medium heat. Bring to the boil, then reduce the heat and simmer for about 8–10 minutes, until the plums are soft and breaking up and the liquid has reduced. Remove from the heat and let cool.

To make the meringue, put the egg whites in a large, clean and dry bowl. Using an electric hand whisk set on medium speed, whisk them until fluffy, then slowly add the sugar, a little at a time, whisking continuously as you go. Once all the sugar has been incorporated into the egg whites, add the lemon juice, cornflour/cornstarch and ground cardamom and whisk for a further 30 seconds, just until it's all been incorporated and you have a stiff and glossy consistency.

Spoon a round of meringue onto the prepared baking sheet, using the circle you have drawn as a guide. Sweep the centre of the meringue to create a small well – you want the sides to be at least 7.5 cm/3 inches high before cooking.

Transfer to the preheated oven and bake for 1 hour, then turn off the oven and leave the meringue inside for 1–2 hours (depending on your oven) to cool.

Carefully lift the cooled meringue and put it on a serving board. Whip the cream and vanilla extract until stiff, then use to fill the centre of the meringue. Top with the plums, pouring the sauce over the top, letting it spill down the sides.

RASPBERRY & VANILLA CREAM FILO 'SHARER' WITH SALTED CHOCOLATE GANACHE

My take on the classic mille-feuille is made of sheets of crisp and light filo/phyllo, layered with vanilla cream and chocolate ganache. As it's fragile, it's best to make all the components first and then assemble it on the board. It gets nice and messy once you start cutting into it...

SERVES 6

200 g/7 oz. ready-made filo/phyllo
    pastry
50 g/3½ tablespoons butter
35 g/4 tablespoons icing/confectioners'
    sugar, plus extra for dusting
150 g/1 cup fresh raspberries
a handful of small mint leaves

VANILLA CREAM
200 ml/scant 1 cup double/heavy cream
1 tablespoon icing/confectioners' sugar
1 vanilla pod/bean

SALTED CHOCOLATE GANACHE
200 ml/scant 1 cup double/heavy
    cream
a few generous pinches of sea salt flakes
1 tablespoon caster/granulated sugar
100 g/3½ oz. dark/bittersweet chocolate
    (75% cocoa solids), broken into pieces
50 g/3½ tablespoons butter, cubed
1–2 tablespoons milk (if needed)

a pastry brush
2 baking sheets, 1 lined with baking
    parchment
an electric hand whisk
2 disposable piping/pastry bags

Preheat the oven to 180°C (350°F) Gas 4.

Cut the filo/phyllo pastry dough into 15 sheets all the same size, about 25 x 15 cm/10 x 6 inches (give or take).

Put the butter and icing/confectioners' sugar in a small saucepan and melt over a low heat until combined. Brush a sheet of pastry with the sweetened butter and lay another sheet neatly on top, repeat this process until you have a stack of five sheets – there is no need to butter the top sheet.

Start a new stack and continue until you have three stacks of five sheets of pastry. Place the stacks of pastry on the lined baking sheet, place another piece of baking parchment over the top of the pastry and lay a second baking sheet on top to keep it flat. (You may need to do this in batches to cook all three piles.)

Bake in the preheated oven for 15 minutes until golden and crisp, then carefully remove the cooked stacks of filo/phyllo and leave to cool on a wire rack. Once completely cooled, keep crisp in an airtight container until ready to use.

To make the vanilla cream, pour the double/heavy cream in to a bowl and sift in the icing/confectioners' sugar. Split the vanilla pod/bean with the tip of a sharp knife and scrape the seeds into the bowl. Use an electric hand whisk to whip until soft peaks form, but be very careful not to overwhip and split your cream. Spoon into a piping/pastry bag and chill in the fridge until ready to use.

To make the chocolate ganache, pour the cream into a heavy-based saucepan along with the salt and the sugar, set over low heat slowly and bring to the boil. As soon as it bubbles, remove from the heat, add the chocolate and butter and beat vigorously with a wooden spoon, if the mixture starts to split, add the milk and continue beating. Spoon the ganache into a piping/pastry bag and chill in the fridge until ready to use.

When ready to assemble, dot your serving dish (or sharing board) with a little chocolate ganache and place the first stack of pastry on top. Pipe a line of cream around the edge of the pastry and then stud with raspberries and little pockets of mint leaves to create a 'wall'. Randomly pipe a few piles of cream in the centre and add a few raspberries. Place the second stack of pastry on top.

Repeat, except this time use the chocolate ganache instead of the cream and again stud with raspberries and mint leaves. Scatter some salt flakes over the chocolate ganache and place the final stack of pastry on top, dust liberally with icing/confectioners' sugar and you are ready to serve with plenty of spoons.

FIGS BAKED IN ALMOND LIQUEUR WITH YOGURT WHIP & FRESH THYME

Baked figs in boozy almond liqueur, nestling in luxurious whipped Greek yogurt with mascarpone, drizzled with their own syrupy thyme-infused juices and topped with a few toasted almonds for crunch. What's not to like here...?

SERVES 6

2 tablespoons flaked/slivered almonds
6 ripe fresh figs
a few sprigs of fresh thyme
2½ tablespoons almond-flavoured
    liqueur, such as Amaretto di Saronno
1 tablespoon clear, runny honey
1 tablespoon caster/granulated sugar

a few drops of pure vanilla extract
½ teaspoon freshly squeezed lemon
    juice
a tiny pinch of fine salt
250 g/scant 1¼ cups thick Greek yogurt
100 g/½ cup mascarpone
1 tablespoon icing/confectioners' sugar

Preheat the oven to 180°C (350°F) Gas 4.

Put the almonds on a dry baking sheet and toast them in the preheated oven for about 5 minutes, until just golden. Remove from the oven, tip off the sheet onto a plate and leave to cool.

Cut each fig in half and arrange them, cut-side up, in an ovenproof baking dish. They should fit quite snugly and not roll around. Break up the sprigs of thyme and tuck them in between the figs.

Put the almond liqueur, honey, sugar, ½ tablespoon water, vanilla extract, lemon juice and salt in a small bowl and whisk until combined. Drizzle the mixture over the figs and thyme. Transfer to the preheated oven and bake for 20 minutes, then remove and set aside to cool.

Put the yogurt, mascarpone and icing/confectioners' sugar in a mixing bowl and beat with a wooden spoon until well combined and fluffy in texture – you can add a dash of milk just to loosen the mixture if it's too thick.

Spoon the yogurt whip on the serving board and use the back of a large spoon to wipe a dent in it. Arrange the figs in groups in the dent and drizzle the syrupy cooking juices over the top. Scatter over the toasted flaked/slivered almonds just before serving.

CITRUS SALAD WITH ROSEWATER CARAMEL

This is a beautiful dessert. Colourful slices of citrus fruits drenched in a fragrant rosewater caramel syrup and topped with crunchy pistachios and dark chocolate shavings. I've included a red grapefruit as I love the bitter sharpness, but you can leave it out, if preferred.

SERVES 6

2 blood oranges
2 oranges
1 red or pink grapefruit (optional)
2 kiwi fruit, gold if you can find these
12 small fresh mint leaves
40 g/⅓ cup pistachio nuts, lightly crushed
1 tablespoon dried edible rose petals, lightly crushed

a 40-g/1½-oz. bar of dark/bittersweet chocolate, chilled
thick Greek yogurt, to serve

ROSEWATER CARAMEL SYRUP
150 ml/⅔ cup warm water
200 g/1 cup caster/superfine sugar
1 cinnamon stick
30 g/2 tablespoons butter
a small pinch of salt
1 tablespoon rosewater

Top and tail all the fruit and then hold each piece, one of the cut-sides down, on a flat surface and use a sharp knife to slice away all the peel and pith (or kiwi skin) from the outside to reveal the flesh. Turn each piece on its side and cut the fruit into thin (just under 5-mm/¼-inch) slices. Arrange the slices on a large, flat platter – I prefer a white one as it works best visually.

To make the rosewater syrup, put half the warm water in a small saucepan with the sugar and cinnamon stick and set over a very low heat. Stir gently until the sugar has dissolved, then turn up the heat and stop stirring. (I mean it, stop stirring or it'll start to crystallize.) Swirl the pan as it turns a blonde colour and starts to caramelize (this will take about 5 minutes), at which point take the pan off the heat and beat in the butter, rapidly followed by the remaining water. Keep beating until both are fully incorporated, then add the salt and return the pan to a very low heat. Bring to a simmer for 2 minutes, remove from the heat and once it's stopped bubbling, stir in the rosewater. Pour the warm syrup over the prepared fruit platter, scatter over the mint leaves, pistachios and rose petals and use a vegetable peeler to shave a little chocolate over the top. Serve with Greek yogurt on the side (or add a few dollops to the platter before garnishing).

STICKY CHOCOLATE & DATE CAKE

No sweet board would be complete without a chocolate fix and this cake does the job nicely. The olive oil keeps it incredibly moist and unctuous (you could say rich, but unctuous is just such a much more attractive word), and a light dusting of icing/confectioners' sugar and a few fresh berries on the top make a welcome addition. I like to cut this ready for people to pick up a slice straight from the board.

SERVES 8

150 g/generous 1 cup stoned/pitted dates
150 ml/²/₃ cup boiling water
40 g/scant ½ cup unsweetened/Dutch process cocoa powder
160 ml/scant ¾ cup fruity olive oil
160 g/generous ¾ cup caster/white granulated sugar
½ teaspoon salt

1 teaspoon freshly squeezed lemon juice
3 eggs, lightly beaten with a fork
icing/confectioners' sugar, for dusting
sprigs of fresh redcurrants, to garnish

an electric hand-held whisk
a 23-cm/9-inch round cake pan, base lined with baking parchment and sides lightly oiled

Finely chop the dates and put them in a heatproof bowl. Pour in the boiling water and leave them to soften for 5 minutes. Sift in the cocoa powder and mix until combined.

Put the olive oil, sugar, salt, lemon juice and eggs in a large mixing bowl and beat together with an electric hand whisk. Slowly pour in the chocolate and date mixture and continue beating until fully combined.

Pour the cake batter into the prepared cake pan. Bake in the preheated oven for 35–40 minutes, or until a knife comes out clean when inserted into the middle of the cake.

Leave to cool before dusting with icing/confectioners' sugar and garnish with sprig of redcurrants, or any other fresh berries you fancy, before serving.

PISTACHIO & CHERRY STUDDED CHOCOLATE TABLET WITH ROSE & TURMERIC

This is a great way to use up chocolate, especially after Easter! Essentially, it is melted chocolate poured onto baking parchment and left to set. But the secret is what you add to it. Here, I've gone with what I enjoy– pistachios, dried cherries and rose petals, but you can top it with whatever you fancy: peanuts, dried cranberries, marshmallows, cookie crumbs, even chilli/hot red pepper flakes, the list is endless.

SERVES 8 TO SHARE

300 g/10½ oz. dark/bittersweet chocolate (70% min cocoa solids)
freshly ground black pepper, to taste
150 g/5½ oz. white chocolate
½ teaspoon caster/granulated sugar
a pinch of ground turmeric
1 tablespoon pistachio nuts, lightly crushed
1 tablespoon dried cherries
1 teaspoon dried edible rose petals
a pinch of sea salt flakes

Set up a bain marie. To do this, bring a medium-sized saucepan half-full of water to a simmer and set a heatproof bowl over it, ensuring the base of the bowl doesn't touch the surface of the water. Break up the dark/bittersweet chocolate, drop it into the bowl and add half a turn of coarsely ground black pepper (you only want a tiny bit) and stir with a wooden spoon until fully melted.

Pour the melted chocolate onto a sheet of baking parchment set on a tray and smooth it out with a spatula to a rectangle roughly 25 x 15 cm/10 x 6 inches.

Take a clean heatproof bowl and melt the white chocolate as you did the dark/bittersweet. Drizzle half of this over one half of the dark/bittersweet chocolate.

Add the sugar and the turmeric to the remaining melted white chocolate still in the bowl. Mix together until the chocolate turns golden and then drizzle this over the other half of the dark/bittersweet chocolate.

Use a cocktail stick/toothpick or the handle of a teaspoon to swirl the three chocolates together to create a pretty marbling effect, less is more in this instance. While it's still warm, scatter over the pistachios, cherries and rose petals, and place in the fridge to set for at least 1 hour. When you are ready to serve, season with a pinch of sea salt flakes. I like to serve just out of the fridge so that it makes a satisfying 'crack' when you break it.

COLOURED SUGAR SYRUPS

A good sugar syrup can be used like paint to add a vibrant dash of colour and sweetness to any dessert board. The method and ingredients for each is basically the same, with only minor tweaks needed to create incredibly varied colours and fragrances. This recipe isn't an exact science – I tend to make them thicker to begin with and water them down a little as needed.

MAKES 250 ML/1 CUP

200 g/1 cup caster/superfine sugar
a few drops of freshly squeezed lemon
  juice
a pinch of salt

VARIATIONS
Kiss-me-quick-red – 1 tablespoon dried
  edible hibiscus flowers
Blushing pink – 2 tablespoons dried
  edible rose petals, plus 1 teaspoon
  rosewater
Baby blue – 1 tablespoon dried edible
  butterfly pea flowers
Hazy green – 1 green tea teabag

For all the variations, start by steeping your chosen variation ingredient in just over 125 ml/$\frac{1}{2}$ cup hot water for about 6 minutes. (Note: if you want a lighter blue, don't steep the butterfly pea flowers, pop them into the saucepan from the start.)

Pass the steeping liquid through a sieve/strainer into a saucepan and add the sugar and the pinch of salt. Set over a medium heat and bring to the boil, then reduce the heat to a simmer and cook for a few minutes, until the mixture thickens slightly.

Remove from the heat, add a few of drops of lemon juice (or the rosewater if making the blushing pink variation) and leave the syrup to cool before using.

Get creative and drizzle, splash or spoon the syrups over your sweets and desserts boards as desired.

INDEX

ACKNOWLEDGEMENTS

Before I get started on the long list of people who I owe a debt of gratitude to for helping me bring this book to life; I want to thank my beautiful wife Anna; your patience is unwavering (yes, even when you've made it clear that should I make the same thing for dinner for a fifth night in a row to get it 'just right' you will scream). Thank you for your support and love – I couldn't do any of this without you.

My children, you bunch of gorgeous lunatics, thank you for also eating the same thing every night for a week (albeit you are slightly more vocal with regards to your patience threshold... i.e. you have none!) Eva, Lex and Luca – I love you guys.

To Cindy Richards, thank you for letting me loose on a second book with Ryland Peters & Small; I'm always humbled by your belief in me and always thrilled to be working with you. Julia Charles, with our first book together, Orexi!, I thought you had mastered the art of black magic in making me sound borderline eloquent. I've now come to realise you are simply the most talented editor (and most sophisticated drinking companion) I've ever met – thank you. Negroni?

To the incredible masters of design and photographic alchemy; Leslie Harrington and Sonya Nathoo for letting me pretend I know what I'm doing, Kathy Kordalis for painstakingly recreating every single recipe for photography with her natural flair (I'm so jealous), Olivia Wardle for sourcing such amazing props, and of course Mowie Kay the genius behind the camera; I'm forever grateful for the gorgeous photography and always denying that you touch up photos of me (thank you, my vanity appreciates it). You guys. Awesome.

I also owe Jean-Christophe Novelli a debt of gratitude for taking the time to stretch the truth about my abilities and write the fabulous Foreword to this book; you've always been an inspiration and great fun to work with; merci beaucoup mon ami.

As with all my books; it's a culmination of inspiration from friends, family, and my brothers Stephan and Marcus, followed by some notorious lunches and dinners where I test my creations back on them; there are too many friends to mention; but you know who you are and I thank you all.

I started these acknowledgements with someone I could never fail to thank; my wife, and I'll end with the same; to my mum and dad; I love you both for everything and now as a parent I understand what a pain in the ass I was as a kid, I'll always be indebted to you. Seriously, I'll pay you back I promise.

Theo x